React Portfolio App Development

Increase your online presence and create your personal brand

Abdelfattah Ragab

React Portfolio App Development

Increase your online presence and create your personal brand

Abdelfattah Ragab

Introduction

Welcome to the book "React Portfolio App Development".

In this book, I will show you how to create an online portfolio application using the React library.

An online portfolio is an important step in your professional career.

By the end of this book, you will have hands-on training in React and end up with a beautiful portfolio that you can use in your career. Create your own brand, impress your potential employers and show the world your skills. Let us go!

Source code

The source code is available on the book website

https://books.abdelfattah-ragab.com

Chapter 1: Project Preview

1.1 Pages

The project contains the following pages:

- Home
- About
- CV
- Projects
- Contact

1.2 Preview (Mobile)

About

I am Abdelfattah Ragab, a Senior Software Developer with extensive experience of over 20 years in the field. My expertise lies in frontend technologies, with a particular focus on the Angular framework.

Throughout my career, I have honed my skills and knowledge to become proficient in creating exceptional user interfaces and crafting seamless web experiences. My passion for frontend development drives me to stay up-to-date with the latest tools and techniques, enabling me to deliver high-quality solutions to complex problems.

With a proven track record of successful projects, I am recognized for my professionalism, attention to detail, and commitment to achieving outstanding results.

CV

Senior Software Developer - Angular

2019 - Present

Working for clients online:

- Lead Angular teams
- Perform application analysis
- Create architecture of the applications
- Develop the Angular applications

Senior Software Developer - Java/Angular

2017 - 2019

Work for the company siParadigm:

- Develop the backend system using Java
- Develop the customer portal with Angular
- Optimize the complex SQL queries
- Create PDF and Word reports

Abdelfattah Ragab
Projects
HOTEL BOOKING
ONLINE
JUST FOR
NEW ARRIVAL
FOR ONLINE 50% OFF

Contact

Giza, Giza Governorate, Egypt

Abdelfattah Ragab

1.3 Preview (Desktop)

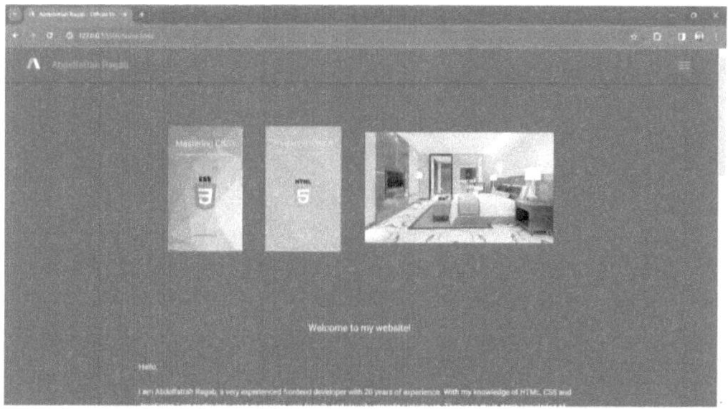

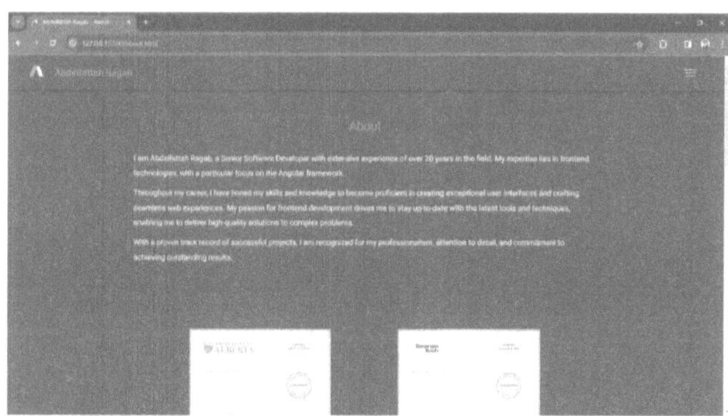

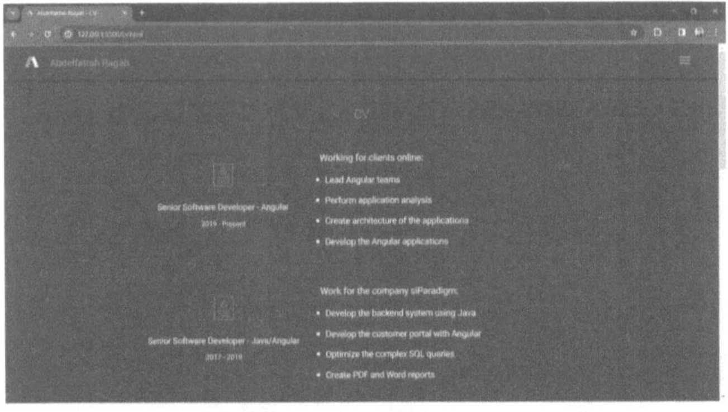
Abdelfattah Ragab
CV
Senior Software Developer - Angular
2019 - Present
Working for clients online:
Lead Angular teams
Perform application analysis
Create architecture of the applications
Develop the Angular applications
Senior Software Developer - Java/Angular
2017 - 2019
Work for the company stParadigm:
Develop the backend system using Java
Develop the customer portal with Angular
Optimize the complex SQL queries
Create PDF and Word reports

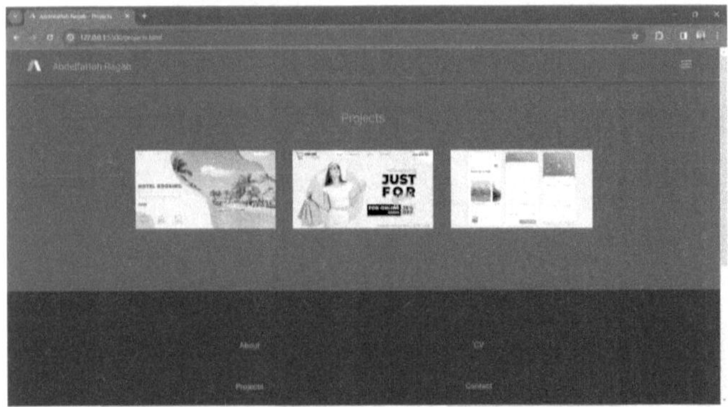
Abdelfattah Ragab
Projects
JUST FOR
About
CV
Projects
Contact

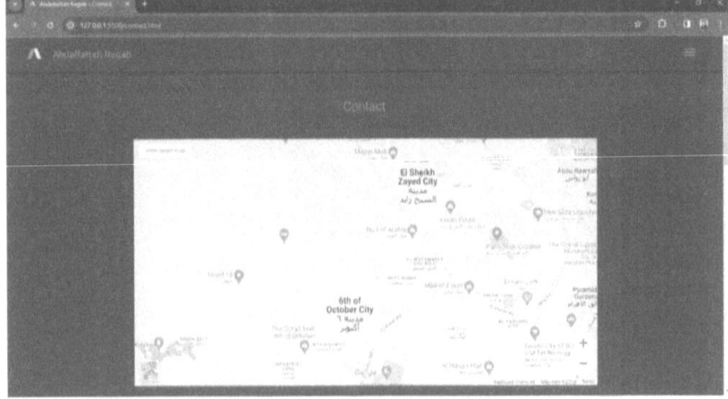
Abdelfattah Ragab
Contact
El Sheikh
Zayed City
6th of
October City

1.4 Your Own Brand

Use the Huemint website to help you choose your brand colors.

https://huemint.com

Chapter 2: App Layout

2.1 App Diagram

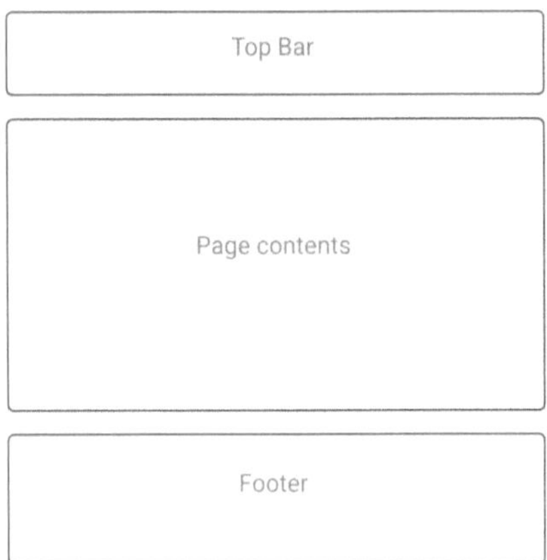

2.2 App Structure

```
<TopBar />
<Sidenav />
<main className="main">
  <Routes></Routes>
</main>
<Footer />
```

2.3 App Folder Structure

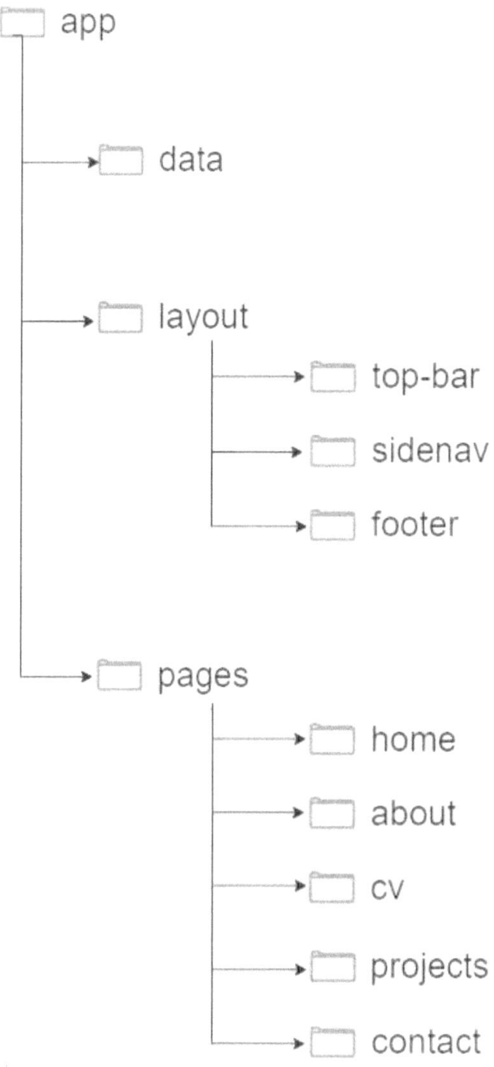

Chapter 3: Project Setup

3.1 Create the App

```
npm create vite@latest
```

Project name: **portfolio-app**

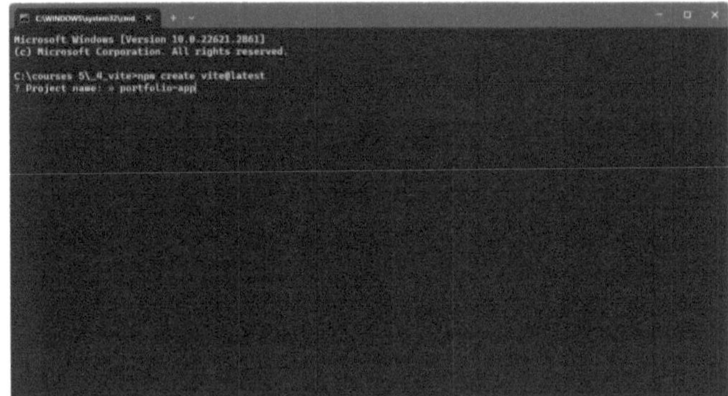

Select a framework: **React**

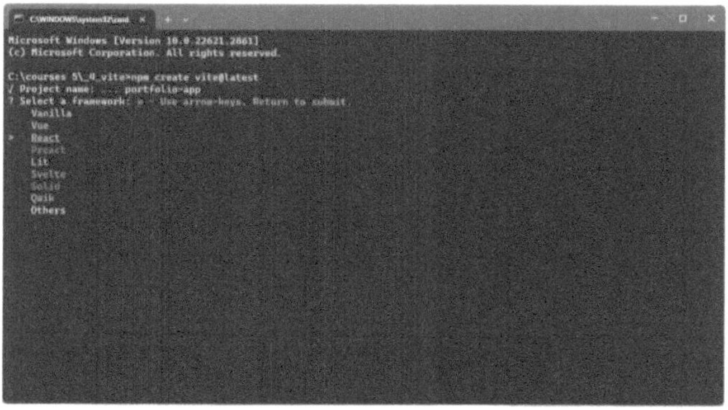

Select a variant: **TypeScript**

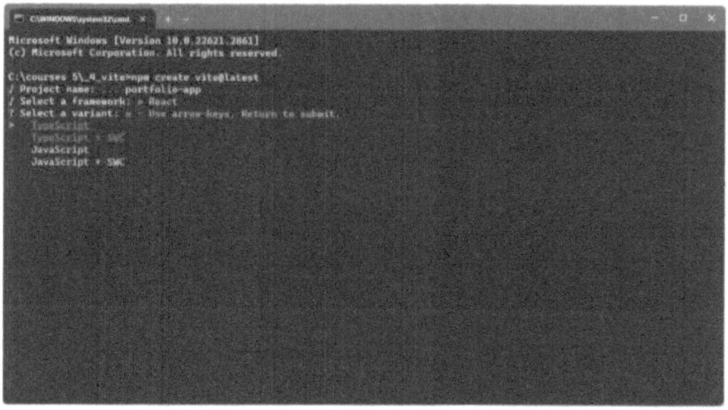

Done.

Open it in VS Code

Run

```
npm install
```

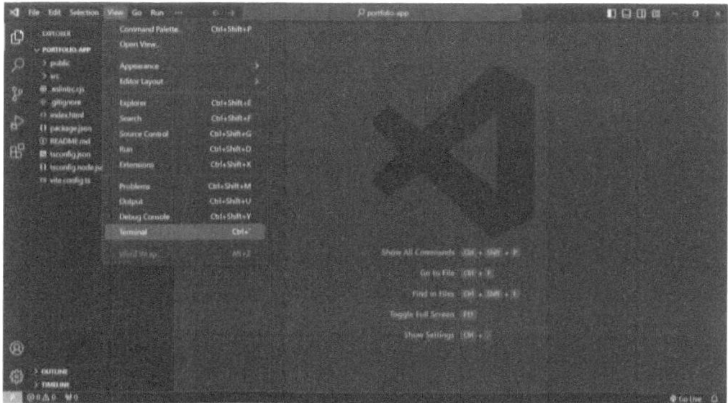

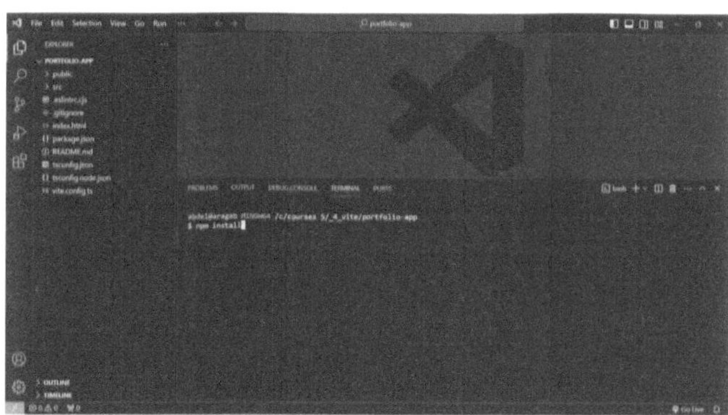

Done

3.2 Install React Router

npm install react-router-dom

3.3 Run the App

```
npm run dev
```

Ready

Open the browser at http://localhost:5173/

Vite + React

count is 0

Edit src/App.tsx and save to test HMR

Click on the Vite and React logos to learn more

3.4 Copy the Assets

Paste the project assets to the "public" folder.

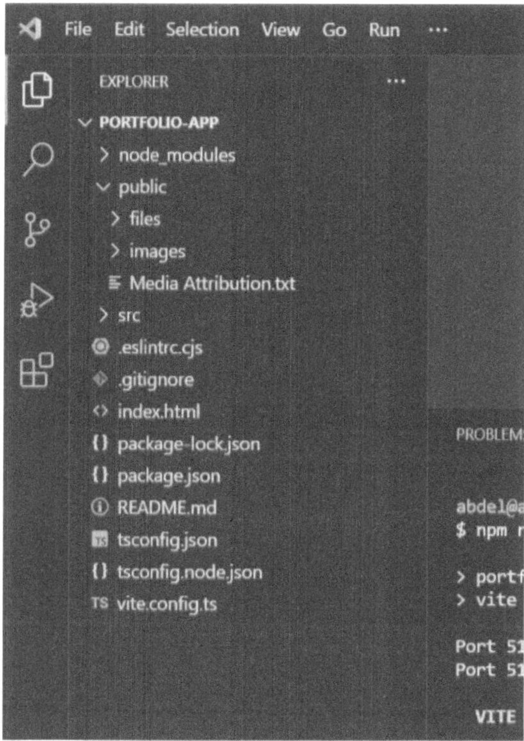

3.5 Clean the app

1. Remove everything inside the App.tsx and keep only the function as follows

```tsx
import "./App.css";


function App() {
  return <></>;
}


export default App;
```

```tsx
1  import "./App.css";
2
3  function App() {
4    return <></>;
5  }
6
7  export default App;
```

2. Add react router

```tsx
import "./App.css";
import { BrowserRouter, Routes } from
"react-router-dom";


function App() {
  return (
    <div>
      <BrowserRouter>
        <main className="main">
```

```
      <Routes></Routes>
    </main>
  </BrowserRouter>
</div>
);
}


export default App;
```

```
1   import "./App.css";
2   import { BrowserRouter, Routes } from "react-router-dom";
3
4   function App() {
5     return (
6       <div>
7         <BrowserRouter>
8           <main className="main">
9             <Routes></Routes>
10          </main>
11        </BrowserRouter>
12      </div>
13    );
14  }
15
16  export default App;
```

3. Remove everything in App.css

4. Remove everything in index.css

You should now have a white page that looks like this

3.6 Set Title and Icon

In the index.html file.

1. Set app title

```
<title>Portfolio App</title>
```

```
5    <title>Portfolio App</title>
```

2. Set app icon

```
<link rel="icon" type="image/x-icon"
href="images/logo.png" />
```

```
5    <link rel="icon" type="image/x-icon" href="images/logo.png" />
```

3.7 Add Global Style

Add the following to index.css

```css
* {
  margin: 0;
  padding: 0;
  box-sizing: border-box;
}
:root {
  --main-color: #1c4270;
  --accent-color-1: #dc5261;
  --accent-color-2: #f8f4a6;


  --footer-background: #0a2444;
  --footer-text: rgba(248, 244, 166, 0.7);
}
html,
body {
  font-family: Roboto, Arial, Helvetica,
sans-serif;
  color: var(--accent-color-2);
  background-color: var(--accent-color-1);
  line-height: 1.5rem !important;
  min-height: 100%;
  position: relative;
  overflow-x: hidden;
}
body {
  background-color: var(--main-color);
```

```css
}
.link {
  cursor: pointer;
  color: var(--accent-color-1);
  text-decoration: none;
}
a:link,
a:visited,
.link:link,
.link:visited {
  color: var(--accent-color-1);
  text-decoration: none;
}
.link:hover,
a:hover {
  filter: brightness(1.1);
}
.main {
  margin: auto;
  padding: 100px 40px;
  @media (min-width: 760px) {
    width: 70%;
    padding: 120px 40px;
  }
}
.main-title {
```

```css
  font-size: 26px;
  font-weight: 300;
  text-align: center;
  color: var(--accent-color-1);
  padding-top: 10px;
  padding-bottom: 30px;
}
```

```css
* {
  margin: 0;
  padding: 0;
  box-sizing: border-box;
}
:root {
  --main-color: #1c4270;
  --accent-color-1: #dc5261;
  --accent-color-2: #f8f4a6;

  --footer-background: #0a2444;
  --footer-text: rgba(248, 244, 166, 0.7);
}
html,
body {
  font-family: Roboto, Arial, Helvetica, sans-serif;
  color: var(--accent-color-2);
  background-color: var(--accent-color-1);
  line-height: 1.5rem !important;
  min-height: 100%;
  position: relative;
  overflow-x: hidden;
}
body {
  background-color: var(--main-color);
}
.link {
  cursor: pointer;
  color: var(--accent-color-1);
  text-decoration: none;
}
a:link,
a:visited,
.link:link,
.link:visited {
  color: var(--accent-color-1);
  text-decoration: none;
}
.link:hover,
a:hover {
  filter: brightness(1.1);
}
.main {
  margin: auto;
  padding: 100px 40px;
  @media (min-width: 760px) {
    width: 70%;
    padding: 120px 40px;
  }
}
.main-title {
  font-size: 26px;
  font-weight: 300;
  text-align: center;
  color: var(--accent-color-1);
  padding-top: 10px;
  padding-bottom: 30px;
}
```

Chapter 4: Top Bar Component

4.1 Preview

4.2 Create It

- Create the folder "layout"

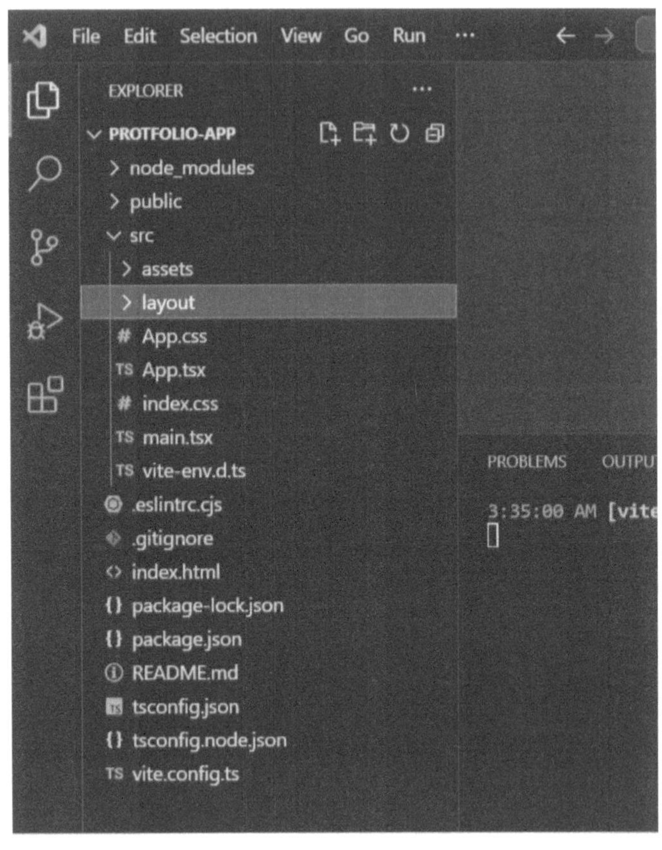

- Create the folder "top-bar" inside "layout"

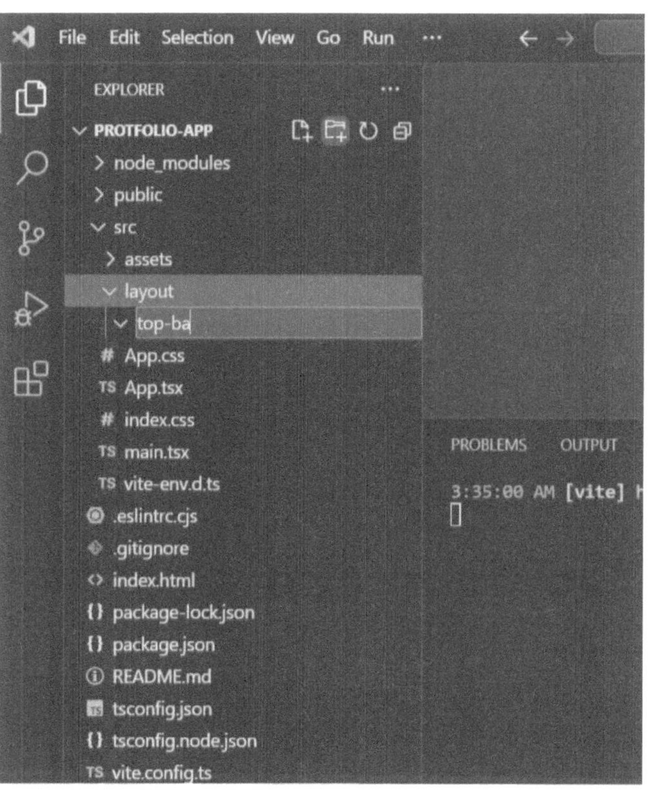
File Edit Selection View Go Run ···
EXPLORER
PROTFOLIO-APP
> node_modules
> public
∨ src
> assets
∨ layout
∨ top-ba
App.css
TS App.tsx
index.css
TS main.tsx
TS vite-env.d.ts
.eslintrc.cjs
.gitignore
<> index.html
{} package-lock.json
{} package.json
README.md
tsconfig.json
{} tsconfig.node.json
TS vite.config.ts
PROBLEMS   OUTPUT
3:35:00 AM [vite]

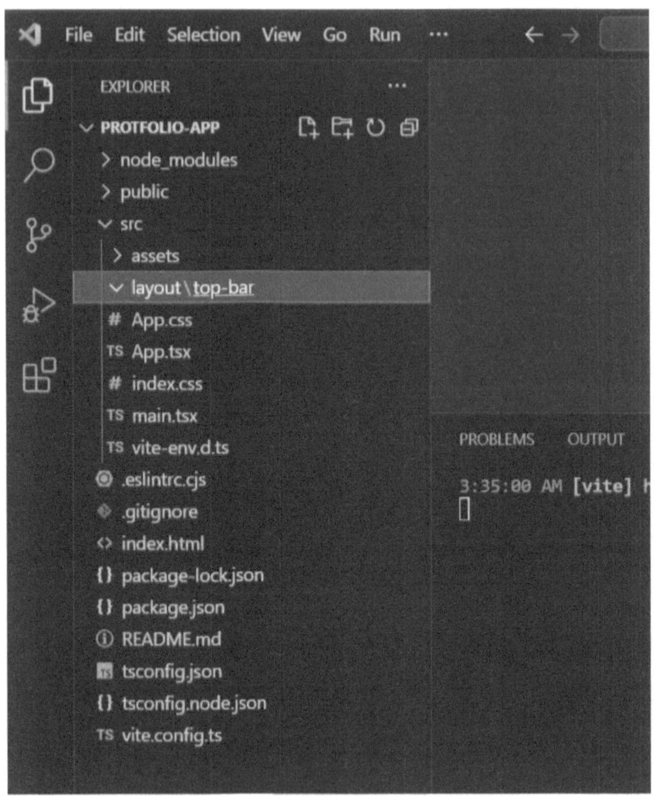

- Create top-bar.tsx
- Create top-bar.css

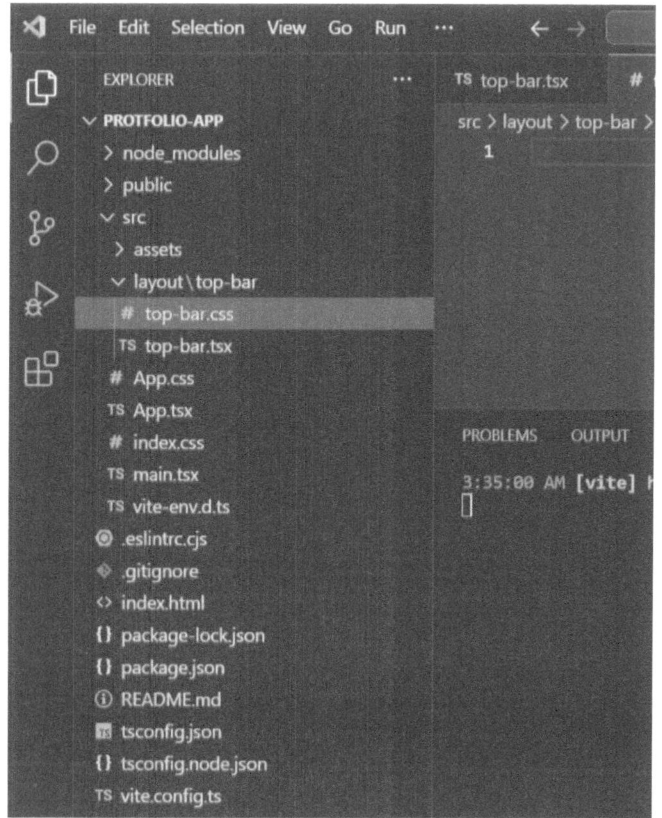

4.3 TSX

```tsx
import "./top-bar.css";

import { Link } from "react-router-dom";

function TopBar() {
  return (
```

```jsx
    <header className="top-bar">
      <div className="brand">
        <Link to="/">
          <img src="images/logo.png" alt="" className="logo link" />
        </Link>
        <Link to="/">
          <div className="brand-name link">Abdelfattah Ragab</div>
        </Link>
      </div>
      <div className="menu-button">
        <img src="images/other/menu.png" alt="" className="menu-icon link" />
      </div>
    </header>
  );
}

export default TopBar;
```

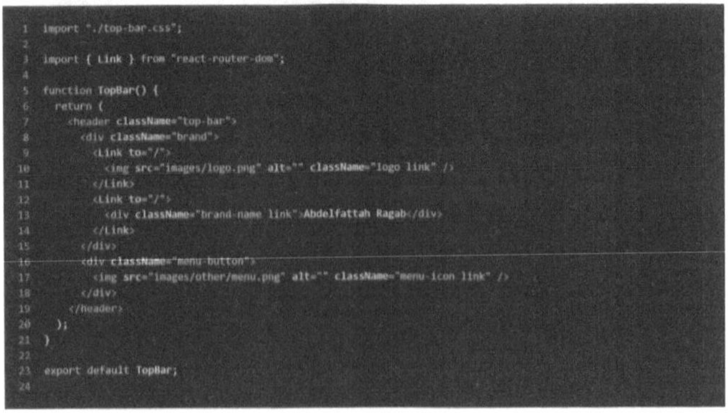

```jsx
1   import "./top-bar.css";
2
3   import { Link } from "react-router-dom";
4
5   function TopBar() {
6     return (
7       <header className="top-bar">
8         <div className="brand">
9           <Link to="/">
10            <img src="images/logo.png" alt="" className="logo link" />
11          </Link>
12          <Link to="/">
13            <div className="brand-name link">Abdelfattah Ragab</div>
14          </Link>
15        </div>
16        <div className="menu-button">
17          <img src="images/other/menu.png" alt="" className="menu-icon link" />
18        </div>
19      </header>
20    );
21  }
22
23  export default TopBar;
24
```

4.4 CSS

```css
.top-bar {
  display: flex;
  width: 100%;
  height: 70px;
  justify-content: space-between;
  align-items: center;
  padding: 10px 20px;
  background-color: var(--main-color);
  color: var(--accent-color-1);
  box-shadow: 0 2px 5px #0000004d;
  position: fixed;
  z-index: 5;
  font-size: 26px;
  @media (min-width: 760px) {
    padding: 10px 40px;
  }
}
.brand {
  display: flex;
  flex-direction: row;
  justify-content: flex-start;
  align-items: center;
  cursor: pointer;
  gap: 20px;
}
.brand-name {
  font-size: 20px;
  padding: 20px 0px;
}
.logo {
  width: 39px;
  height: auto;
```

```css
  display: flex;
  justify-content: center;
  align-items: center;
}
.menu-icon {
  width: 50px;
  padding: 12px;
}
```

```css
1   .top-bar {
2     display: flex;
3     width: 100%;
4     height: 70px;
5     justify-content: space-between;
6     align-items: center;
7     padding: 10px 20px;
8     background-color: var(--main-color);
9     color: var(--accent-color-1);
10    box-shadow: 0 2px 5px #0000004d;
11    position: fixed;
12    z-index: 5;
13    font-size: 26px;
14    @media (min-width: 760px) {
15      padding: 10px 40px;
16    }
17  }
18  .brand {
19    display: flex;
20    flex-direction: row;
21    justify-content: flex-start;
22    align-items: center;
23    cursor: pointer;
24    gap: 20px;
25  }
26  .brand-name {
27    font-size: 20px;
28    padding: 20px 0px;
29  }
30  .logo {
31    width: 39px;
32    height: auto;
33    display: flex;
34    justify-content: center;
35    align-items: center;
36  }
37  .menu-icon {
38    width: 50px;
39    padding: 12px;
40  }
```

4.5 Use It

Use it in App.tsx

```tsx
import "./App.css";
```

```jsx
import { BrowserRouter, Routes } from
"react-router-dom";
import TopBar from "./layout/top-bar/top-bar";

function App() {
  return (
    <div>
      <BrowserRouter>
        <TopBar />
        <main className="main">
          <Routes></Routes>
        </main>
      </BrowserRouter>
    </div>
  );
}

export default App;
```

```jsx
1   import "./App.css";
2   import { BrowserRouter, Routes } from "react-router-dom";
3   import TopBar from "./layout/top-bar/top-bar";
4
5   function App() {
6     return (
7       <div>
8         <BrowserRouter>
9           <TopBar />
10          <main className="main">
11            <Routes></Routes>
12          </main>
13        </BrowserRouter>
14      </div>
15    );
16  }
17
18  export default App;
```

Chapter 5: Sidenav Data

5.1 Create It

Create a new "data" folder

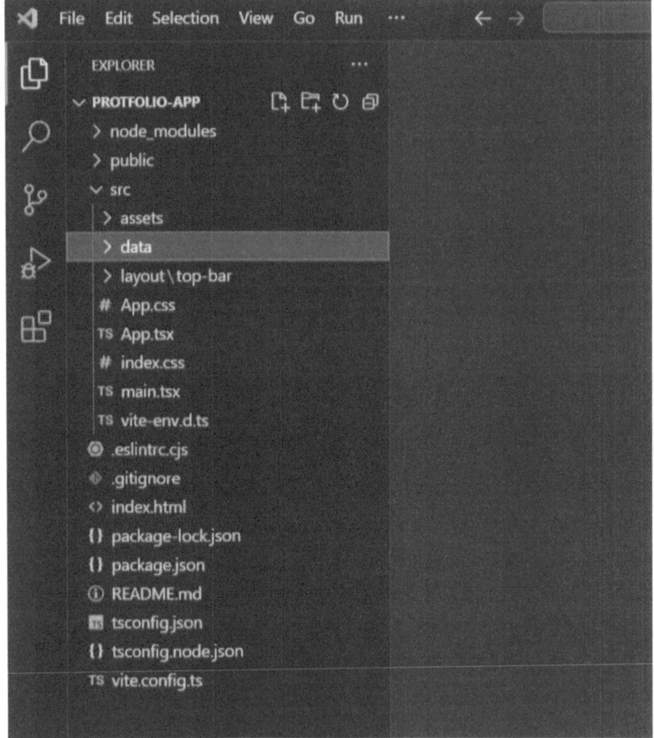

Create the file sidenav.data.ts

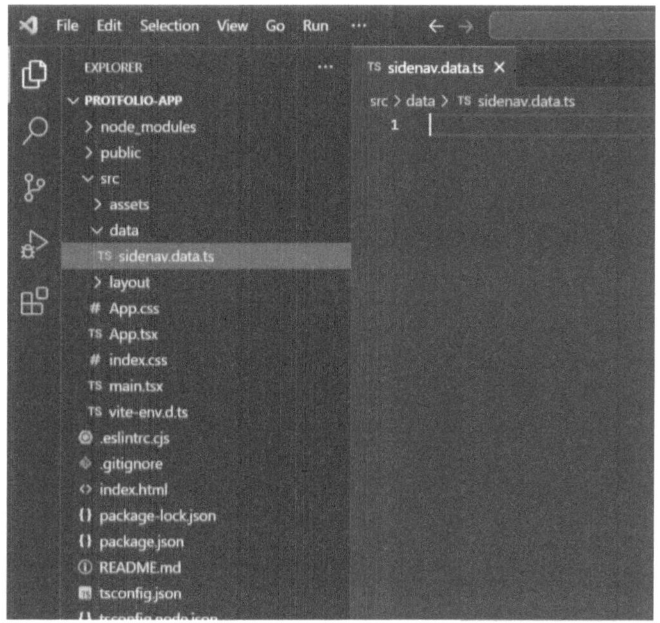

5.2 TS

Here is the TS code of the data file

```ts
export interface SidenavItem {
  title: string;
  path: string;
}

export const SIDENAV_ITEMS: SidenavItem[] = [
  { title: "Home", path: "home" },
  { title: "About", path: "about" },
  { title: "CV", path: "cv" },
  { title: "Projects", path: "projects" },
  { title: "Contact", path: "contact" },
```

];

```
1   export interface SidenavItem {
2     title: string;
3     path: string;
4   }
5
6   export const SIDENAV_ITEMS: SidenavItem[] = [
7     { title: "Home", path: "home" },
8     { title: "About", path: "about" },
9     { title: "CV", path: "cv" },
10    { title: "Projects", path: "projects" },
11    { title: "Contact", path: "contact" },
12  ];
```

Chapter 6: Sidenav Component

6.1 Preview

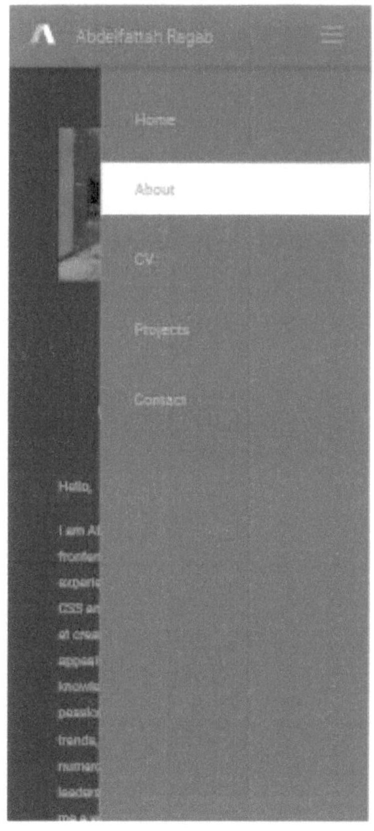

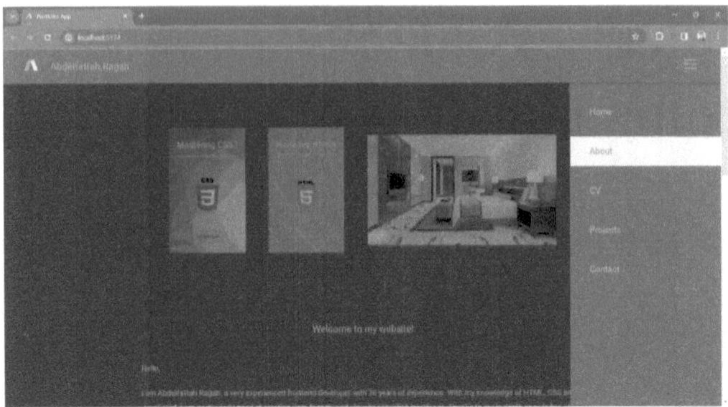

6.2 Create It

- Create a new folder "sidenav" inside the "layout" folder

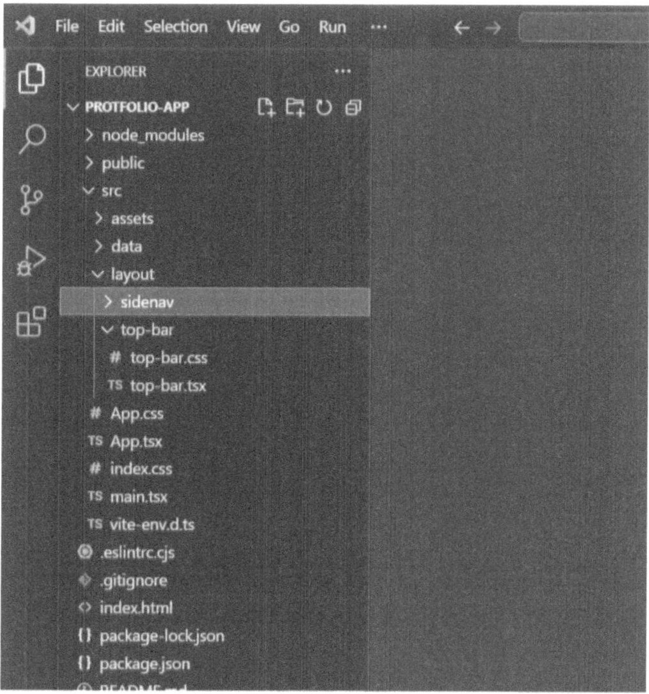

- Create sidenav.tsx
- Create sidenav.css

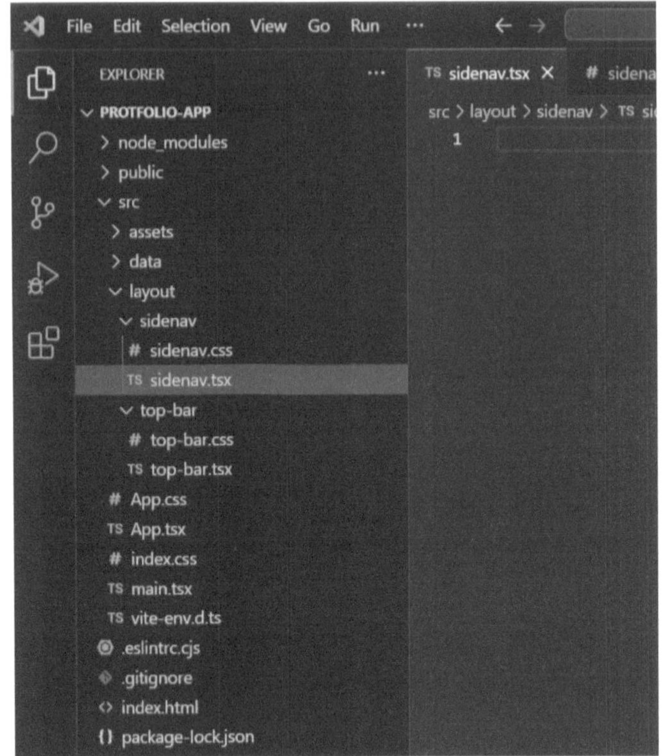

6.3 TSX

```tsx
import { useNavigate } from "react-router-dom";
import { SIDENAV_ITEMS, SidenavItem } from
"../../data/sidenav.data";
import "./sidenav.css";

function Sidenav() {
  const navigate = useNavigate();
```

```tsx
  let opened = false;
  const onItemClicked = (path: string) => {
    navigate(path);
  };
  const createSidenavItem = (item: SidenavItem)
=> (
    <div
      key={item.title}
      onClick={() => onItemClicked(item.path)}
      className="sidenav-item"
    >
      {item.title}
    </div>
  );
  return (
    <>
      <div className={`backdrop ${opened ?
"backdrop-visible" : ""} `}></div>
      <nav className={`sidenav ${opened ?
"sidenav-visible" : ""}`}>
        {SIDENAV_ITEMS.map(createSidenavItem)}
      </nav>
    </>
  );
}

export default Sidenav;
```

```tsx
import { useNavigate } from "react-router-dom";
import { SIDENAV_ITEMS, SidenavItem } from "../../data/sidenav.data";
import "./sidenav.css";

function Sidenav() {
  const navigate = useNavigate();

  let opened = false;
  const onItemClicked = (path: string) => {
    navigate(path);
  };
  const createSidenavItem = (item: SidenavItem) => (
    <div
      key={item.title}
      onClick={() => onItemClicked(item.path)}
      className="sidenav-item"
    >
      {item.title}
    </div>
  );
  return (
    <>
      <div className={`backdrop ${opened ? "backdrop-visible" : ""}`}></div>
      <nav className={`sidenav ${opened ? "sidenav-visible" : ""}`}>
        {SIDENAV_ITEMS.map(createSidenavItem)}
      </nav>
    </>
  );
}

export default Sidenav;
```

6.4 CSS

```css
.backdrop {
  width: 100vw;
  height: 100vh;
  background-color: rgba(0, 0, 0, 0.6);
  position: fixed;
  top: 0;
  left: 0;
  z-index: 3;
  display: none;
}
.backdrop-visible {
  display: block;
}
.sidenav {
  width: 320px;
  height: 100%;
```

```css
  min-height: 100vh;
  box-shadow: 1px 1px 3px 1px gray;
  background-color: var(--main-color);
  display: flex !important;
  flex-direction: column;
  gap: 20px;
  padding-top: 100px;
  position: absolute;
  top: 0px;
  right: -320px;
  transition: all 300ms;
  z-index: 4;
  overflow: hidden;
}
.sidenav-visible {
  right: 0px;
}
.sidenav-item {
  padding: 0px 40px;
  width: 100%;
  height: 60px;
  text-decoration: none;
  display: flex;
  justify-content: flex-start;
  align-items: center;
  font-size: 18px;
  font-weight: 500;
  color: var(--accent-color-1);
  cursor: pointer;
}
.sidenav-item:hover {
  background-color: var(--accent-color-2);
}
```

```css
.backdrop {
  width: 100vw;
  height: 100vh;
  background-color: rgba(0, 0, 0, 0.6);
  position: fixed;
  top: 0;
  left: 0;
  z-index: 3;
  display: none;
}
.backdrop-visible {
  display: block;
}
.sidenav {
  width: 320px;
  height: 100%;
  min-height: 100vh;
  box-shadow: 1px 1px 3px 1px gray;
  background-color: var(--main-color);
  display: flex !important;
  flex-direction: column;
  gap: 20px;
  padding-top: 100px;
  position: absolute;
  top: 0px;
  right: -320px;
  transition: all 300ms;
  z-index: 4;
  overflow: hidden;
}
.sidenav-visible {
  right: 0px;
}
.sidenav-item {
  padding: 0px 40px;
  width: 100%;
  height: 60px;
  text-decoration: none;
  display: flex;
  justify-content: flex-start;
  align-items: center;
  font-size: 18px;
  font-weight: 500;
  color: var(--accent-color-1);
  cursor: pointer;
}
.sidenav-item:hover {
  background-color: var(--accent-color-2);
}
```

6.5 Use It

Use it in App.tsx

```tsx
import "./App.css";
import { BrowserRouter, Routes } from
"react-router-dom";
import TopBar from "./layout/top-bar/top-bar";
import Sidenav from "./layout/sidenav/sidenav";
```

```
function App() {
  return (
    <div>
      <BrowserRouter>
        <TopBar />
        <Sidenav />
        <main className="main">
          <Routes></Routes>
        </main>
      </BrowserRouter>
    </div>
  );
}

export default App;
```

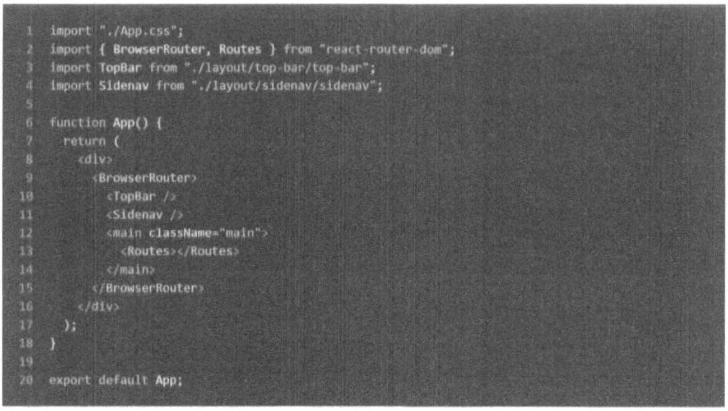

```
1   import "./App.css";
2   import { BrowserRouter, Routes } from "react-router-dom";
3   import TopBar from "./layout/top-bar/top-bar";
4   import Sidenav from "./layout/sidenav/sidenav";
5
6   function App() {
7     return (
8       <div>
9         <BrowserRouter>
10          <TopBar />
11          <Sidenav />
12          <main className="main">
13            <Routes></Routes>
14          </main>
15        </BrowserRouter>
16      </div>
17    );
18  }
19
20  export default App;
```

6.6 Share Sidenav State

Update App.tsx

```
import "./App.css";
import { BrowserRouter, Routes } from
"react-router-dom";
```

```jsx
import TopBar from "./layout/top-bar/top-bar";
import Sidenav from "./layout/sidenav/sidenav";
import { useState } from "react";

function App() {
  const [opened, setOpened] =
useState(false);

  return (
    <div>
      <BrowserRouter>
        <TopBar opened={opened}
setOpened={setOpened} />
        <Sidenav opened={opened}
setOpened={setOpened} />
        <main className="main">
          <Routes></Routes>
        </main>
      </BrowserRouter>
    </div>
  );
}

export default App;
```

```
 1  import "./App.css";
 2  import { BrowserRouter, Routes } from "react-router-dom";
 3  import TopBar from "./layout/top-bar/top-bar";
 4  import Sidenav from "./layout/sidenav/sidenav";
 5  import { useState } from "react";
 6
 7  function App() {
 8    const [opened, setOpened] = useState(false);
 9
10    return (
11      <div>
12        <BrowserRouter>
13          <TopBar opened={opened} setOpened={setOpened} />
14          <Sidenav opened={opened} setOpened={setOpened} />
15          <main className="main">
16            <Routes></Routes>
17          </main>
18        </BrowserRouter>
19      </div>
20    );
21  }
22
23  export default App;
```

Update top-bar.tsx

```tsx
import "./top-bar.css";

import { Link } from "react-router-dom";

type Props = {
  opened: boolean;
  setOpened: any;
};

function TopBar({ opened, setOpened }: Props) {
  function toggleSidenav() {
    setOpened(!opened);
  }
  return (
    <header className="top-bar">
      <div className="brand">
        <Link to="/">
          <img src="images/logo.png" alt="" className="logo link" />
        </Link>
        <Link to="/">
```

```jsx
            <div className="brand-name
link">Abdelfattah Ragab</div>
          </Link>
        </div>
        <div className="menu-button">
          <img
            src="images/other/menu.png"
            onClick={toggleSidenav}
            alt=""
            className="menu-icon link"
          />
        </div>
      </header>
  );
}


export default TopBar;
```

```tsx
1   import "./top-bar.css";
2
3   import { Link } from "react-router-dom";
4
5   type Props = {
6     opened: boolean;
7     setOpened: any;
8   };
9
10  function TopBar({ opened, setOpened }: Props) {
11    function toggleSidenav() {
12      setOpened(!opened);
13    }
14    return (
15      <header className="top-bar">
16        <div className="brand">
17          <Link to="/">
18            <img src="images/logo.png" alt="" className="logo link" />
19          </Link>
20          <Link to="/">
21            <div className="brand-name link">Abdelfattah Ragab</div>
22          </Link>
23        </div>
24        <div className="menu-button">
25          <img
26            src="images/other/menu.png"
27            onClick={toggleSidenav}
28            alt=""
29            className="menu-icon link"
30          />
31        </div>
32      </header>
33    );
34  }
35
36  export default TopBar;
```

Update sidenav.tsx

```tsx
import { useNavigate } from "react-router-dom";
import { SIDENAV_ITEMS, SidenavItem } from
"../../data/sidenav.data";
import "./sidenav.css";

type Props = {
  opened: boolean;
  setOpened: any;
};

function Sidenav({ opened, setOpened }: Props)
{
  const navigate = useNavigate();

  let opened = true;
  const onItemClicked = (path: string) => {
    navigate(path);
    setOpened(false);
  };
  const createSidenavItem = (item: SidenavItem)
=> (
    <div
      key={item.title}
      onClick={() => onItemClicked(item.path)}
      className="sidenav-item"
    >
      {item.title}
    </div>
  );
  return (
    <>
```

```tsx
        <div className={`backdrop ${opened ?
"backdrop-visible" : ""} `}></div>
        <nav className={`sidenav ${opened ?
"sidenav-visible" : ""}`}>
          {SIDENAV_ITEMS.map(createSidenavItem)}
        </nav>
      </>
    );
}

export default Sidenav;
```

```tsx
1   import { useNavigate } from "react-router-dom";
2   import { SIDENAV_ITEMS, SidenavItem } from "../../data/sidenav.data";
3   import "./sidenav.css";
4
5   type Props = {
6     opened: boolean;
7     setOpened: any;
8   };
9
10  function Sidenav({ opened, setOpened }: Props) {
11    const navigate = useNavigate();
12
13    const onItemClicked = (path: string) => {
14      navigate(path);
15      setOpened(false);
16    };
17    const createSidenavItem = (item: SidenavItem) => (
18      <div
19        key={item.title}
20        onClick={() => onItemClicked(item.path)}
21        className="sidenav-item"
22      >
23        {item.title}
24      </div>
25    );
26    return (
27      <>
28        <div className={`backdrop ${opened ? "backdrop-visible" : ""} `}></div>
29        <nav className={`sidenav ${opened ? "sidenav-visible" : ""}`}>
30          {SIDENAV_ITEMS.map(createSidenavItem)}
31        </nav>
32      </>
33    );
34  }
35
36  export default Sidenav;
```

Chapter 7: Footer Component

7.1 Preview

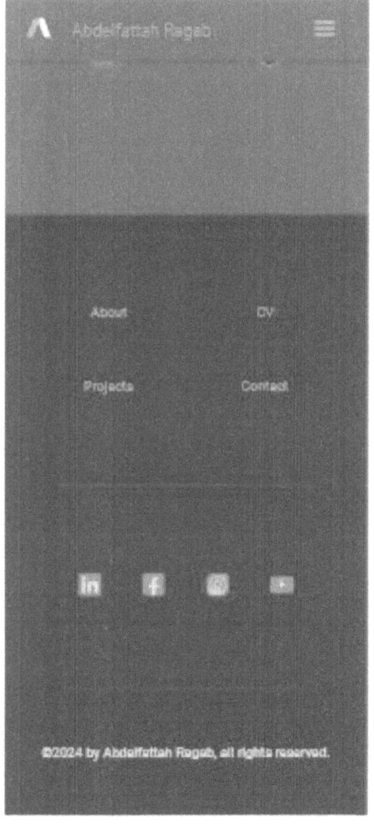

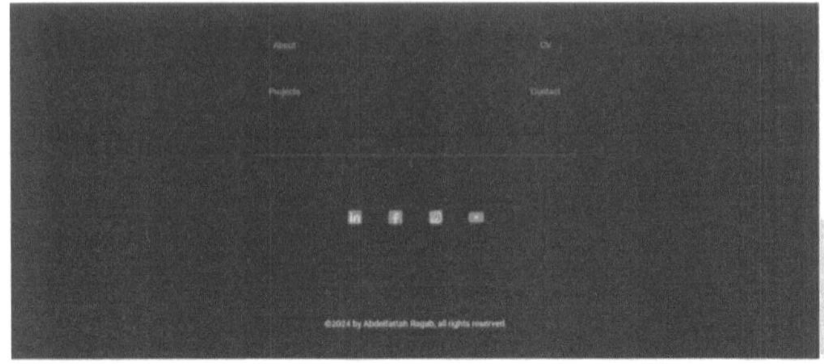

7.2 Create It

- Create a new folder "footer" inside the "layout" folder

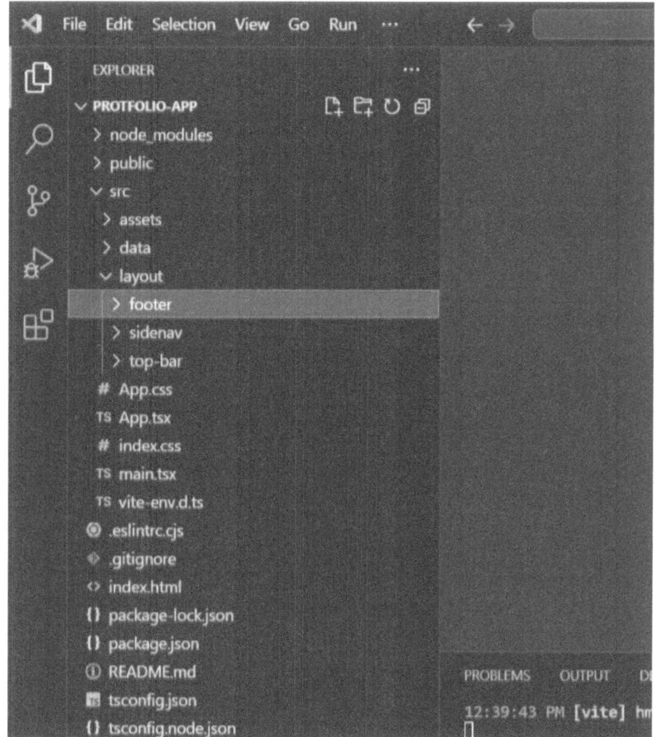

- Create footer.tsx
- Create footer.css

7.3 TSX

```
import "./footer.css";
import { Link } from "react-router-dom";
function Footer() {
  return (
    <footer className="footer">
      <section className="main-footer">
```

```jsx
      <Link to="/about">
        <div className="link">About</div>
      </Link>
      <Link to="/cv">
        <div className="link">CV</div>
      </Link>
      <Link to="/projects">
        <div className="link">Projects</div>
      </Link>
      <Link to="/contact">
        <div className="link">Contact</div>
      </Link>
    </section>
    <div className="divider"></div>
    <section className="social-footer">
      <a href="">
        <img
          src="images/social/linkedin.png"
          alt=""
          className="social-icon"
        />
      </a>
      <a href="">
        <img
          src="images/social/facebook.png"
          alt=""
          className="social-icon"
        />
      </a>
      <a href="">
        <img
          src="images/social/instagram.png"
          alt=""
          className="social-icon"
```

```jsx
        />
      </a>
      <a href="">
        <img
          src="images/social/youtube.png"
          alt=""
          className="social-icon
youtube-icon"
        />
      </a>
    </section>
    <div className="divider"></div>
    <section className="copyright-footer">
      <p>©2024 by Abdelfattah Ragab, all
rights reserved.</p>
    </section>
  </footer>
  );
}

export default Footer;
```

```jsx
1   import "./footer.css";
2   import { Link } from "react-router-dom";
3   function Footer() {
4     return (
5       <footer className="footer">
6         <section className="main-footer">
7           <Link to="/about">
8             <div className="link">About</div>
9           </Link>
10          <Link to="/cv">
11            <div className="link">CV</div>
12          </Link>
13          <Link to="/projects">
14            <div className="link">Projects</div>
15          </Link>
16          <Link to="/contact">
17            <div className="link">Contact</div>
18          </Link>
19        </section>
20        <div className="divider"></div>
21        <section className="social-footer">
22          <a href="">
23            <img
24              src="images/social/linkedin.png"
25              alt=""
26              className="social-icon"
27            />
28          </a>
29          <a href="">
30            <img
31              src="images/social/facebook.png"
32              alt=""
33              className="social-icon"
34            />
35          </a>
36          <a href="">
37            <img
38              src="images/social/instagram.png"
39              alt=""
40              className="social-icon"
41            />
42          </a>
43          <a href="">
44            <img
45              src="images/social/youtube.png"
46              alt=""
47              className="social-icon youtube-icon"
48            />
49          </a>
50        </section>
51        <div className="divider"></div>
52        <section className="copyright-footer">
53          <p>©2024 by Abdelfattah Ragab, all rights reserved.</p>
54        </section>
55      </footer>
56    );
57  }
58
59  export default footer;
```

7.4 CSS

```css
.footer {
  background-color: var(--footer-background);
}
.main-footer {
  padding: 100px 60px;
```

```css
    display: grid;
    grid-template-columns: 1fr 1fr;
    place-items: center center;
    gap: 60px;
    @media (min-width: 760px) {
      padding: 100px 300px;
    }
}
.divider {
  width: 70%;
  height: 1px;
  margin: auto;
  background-color: var(--accent-color-2);
  opacity: 0.1;
  @media (min-width: 760px) {
    width: 40%;
  }
}
.social-footer {
  display: flex;
  gap: 50px;
  justify-content: center;
  padding: 100px 60px;
  align-items: center;
  background-color: var(--footer-background);
}
.social-footer .social-icon {
  width: 26px;
  height: auto;
  opacity: 0.8;
}
.youtube-icon {
  transform: scale(1.12);
}
```

```css
.copyright-footer {
  display: flex;
  justify-content: center;
  align-items: center;
  background-color: var(--footer-background);
  color: var(--footer-text);
  padding: 60px 0;
  cursor: default;
}
```

```css
1   .footer {
2     background-color: var(--footer-background);
3   }
4   .main-footer {
5     padding: 100px 60px;
6     display: grid;
7     grid-template-columns: 1fr 1fr;
8     place-items: center center;
9     gap: 60px;
10    @media (min-width: 760px) {
11      padding: 100px 300px;
12    }
13  }
14  .divider {
15    width: 70%;
16    height: 1px;
17    margin: auto;
18    background-color: var(--accent-color-2);
19    opacity: 0.1;
20    @media (min-width: 760px) {
21      width: 40%;
22    }
23  }
24  .social-footer {
25    display: flex;
26    gap: 50px;
27    justify-content: center;
28    padding: 100px 60px;
29    align-items: center;
30    background-color: var(--footer-background);
31  }
32  .social-footer .social-icon {
33    width: 26px;
34    height: auto;
35    opacity: 0.8;
36  }
37  .youtube-icon {
38    transform: scale(1.12);
39  }
40  .copyright-footer {
41    display: flex;
42    justify-content: center;
43    align-items: center;
44    background-color: var(--footer-background);
45    color: var(--footer-text);
46    padding: 60px 0;
47    cursor: default;
48  }
49
```

7.5 Use It

Use it in App.tsx

```tsx
import "./App.css";
import { BrowserRouter, Routes } from
"react-router-dom";
import TopBar from "./layout/top-bar/top-bar";
import Sidenav from "./layout/sidenav/sidenav";
import { useState } from "react";
import Footer from "./layout/footer/footer";

function App() {
  const [opened, setOpened] = useState(false);

  return (
    <div>
      <BrowserRouter>
        <TopBar opened={opened}
setOpened={setOpened} />
        <Sidenav opened={opened}
setOpened={setOpened} />
        <main className="main">
          <Routes></Routes>
        </main>
        <Footer />
      </BrowserRouter>
    </div>
  );
}

export default App;
```

```jsx
import "./App.css";
import { BrowserRouter, Routes } from "react-router-dom";
import TopBar from "./layout/top-bar/top-bar";
import Sidenav from "./layout/sidenav/sidenav";
import { useState } from "react";
import Footer from "./layout/footer/footer";

function App() {
  const [opened, setOpened] = useState(false);

  return (
    <div>
      <BrowserRouter>
        <TopBar opened={opened} setOpened={setOpened} />
        <Sidenav opened={opened} setOpened={setOpened} />
        <main className="main">
          <Routes></Routes>
        </main>
        <Footer />
      </BrowserRouter>
    </div>
  );
}

export default App;
```

Chapter 8: Home Page

8.1 Preview

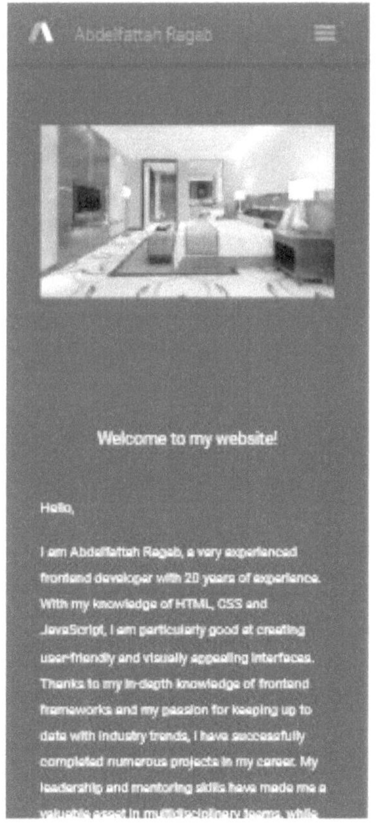

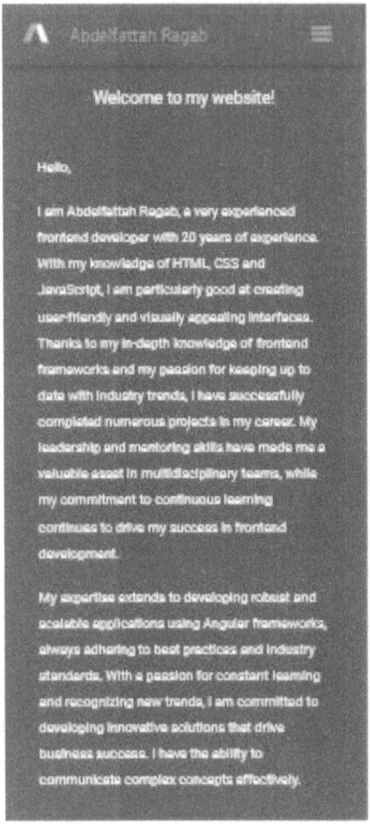

Welcome to my website!

Hello,

I am Abdelfattah Ragab, a very experienced frontend developer with 20 years of experience. With my knowledge of HTML, CSS and JavaScript, I am particularly good at creating user-friendly and visually appealing interfaces. Thanks to my in-depth knowledge of frontend frameworks and my passion for keeping up to date with industry trends, I have successfully completed numerous projects in my career. My leadership and mentoring skills have made me a valuable asset in multidisciplinary teams, while my commitment to continuous learning continues to drive my success in frontend development.

My expertise extends to developing robust and scalable applications using Angular frameworks, always adhering to best practices and industry standards. With a passion for constant learning and recognizing new trends, I am committed to developing innovative solutions that drive business success. I have the ability to communicate complex concepts effectively.

My expertise extends to developing robust and scalable applications using Angular frameworks, always adhering to best practices and industry standards. With a passion for constant learning and recognizing new trends, I am committed to developing innovative solutions that drive business success. I have the ability to communicate complex concepts effectively.

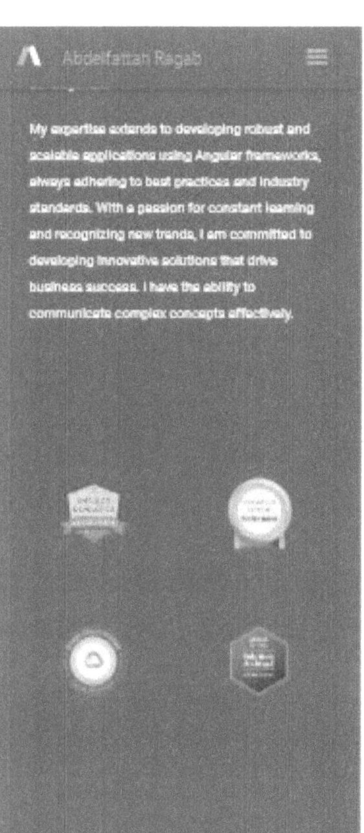

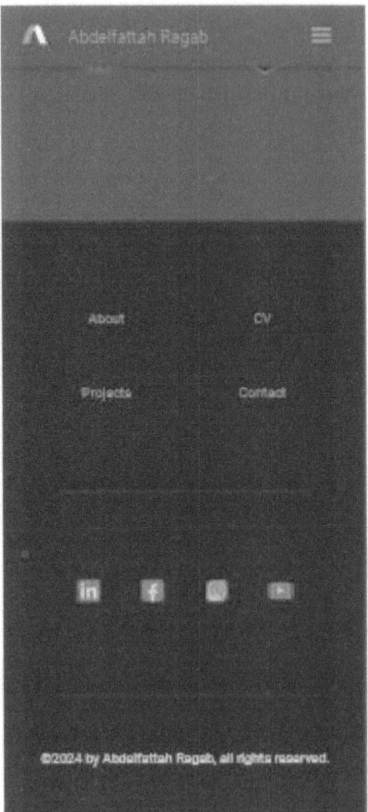
Abdelfattah Ragab
About
CV
Projects
Contact
©2024 by Abdelfattah Ragab, all rights reserved.

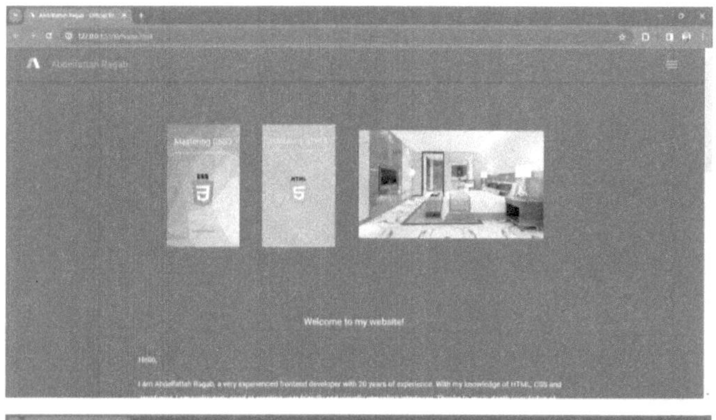

Abdelfattah Ragab
Mastering CSS3
CSS3
Mastering HTML5
HTML5
Welcome to my website!
Hello,
I am AbdelFattah Ragab, a very experienced frontend developer with 20 years of experience. With my knowledge of HTML, CSS and

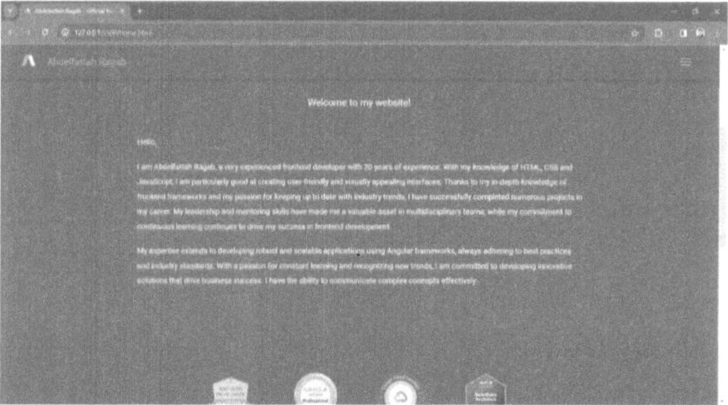

Abdelfattah Ragab
Welcome to my website!
Hello,
I am AbdelFattah Ragab, a very experienced frontend developer with 20 years of experience. With my knowledge of HTML, CSS and
JavaScript, I am particularly good at creating user-friendly and visually appealing interfaces. Thanks to my in-depth knowledge of
frontend frameworks and my passion for keeping up to date with industry trends, I have successfully completed numerous projects in
my career. My leadership and mentoring skills have made me a valuable asset in multidisciplinary teams, while my commitment to
continuous learning continues to drive my success in frontend development.

My expertise extends to developing robust and scalable applications using Angular frameworks, always adhering to best practices
and industry standards. With a passion for constant learning and recognizing new trends, I am committed to developing innovative
solutions that drive business success. I have the ability to communicate complex concepts effectively.

Abdelfattah Ragab
About
CV
Projects
Contact

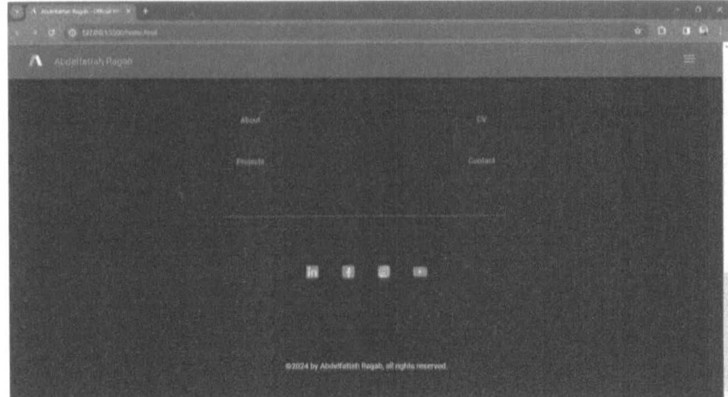

8.2 Page Outline

```
<Promotion />
<Welcome />
<Badges />
```

8.3 Create It

- Create a new folder "pages"
- Create a new folder "home" inside the "pages" folder

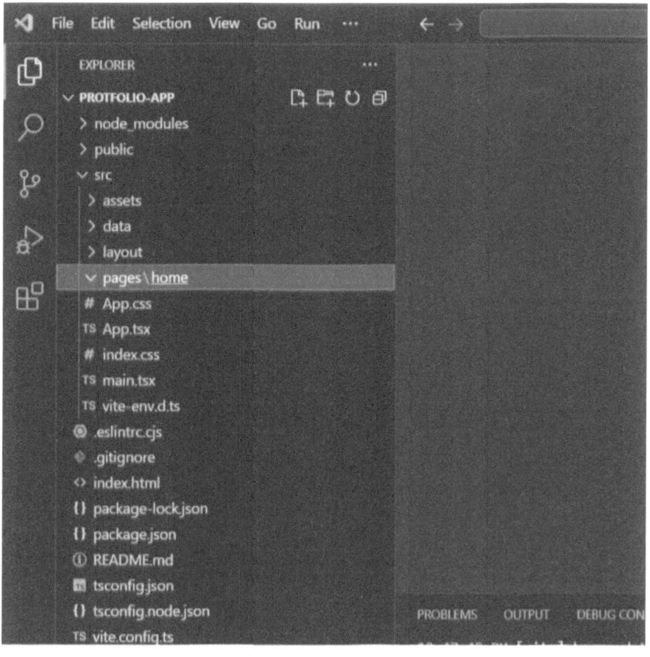

- Create home.tsx
- Create home.css

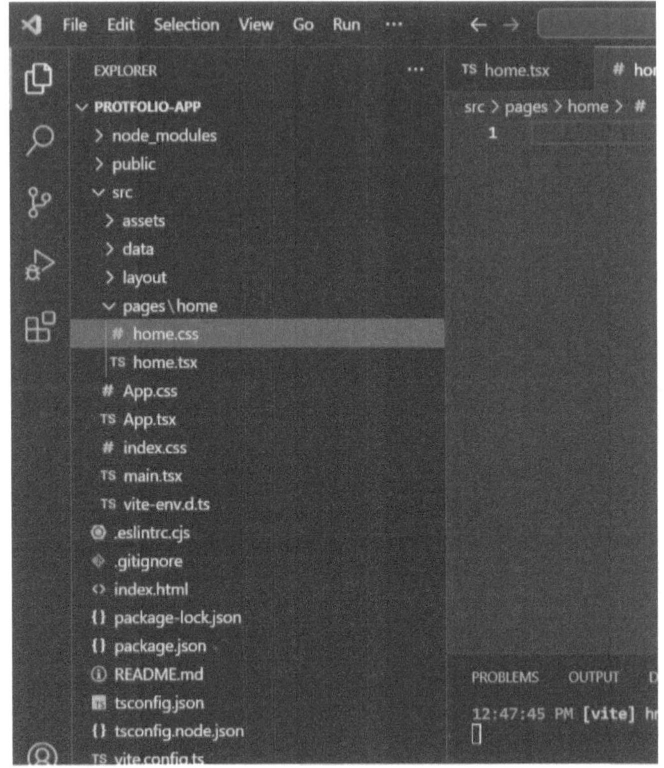

8.4 TSX

```tsx
function Home() {
  return <></>;
}

export default Home;
```

```
1  function Home() {
2    return <></>;
3  }
4
5  export default Home;
```

8.5 CSS

Nothing

8.6 Add Route

Update App.tsx

```
import "./App.css";
import { BrowserRouter, Route, Routes } from
"react-router-dom";
import TopBar from "./layout/top-bar/top-bar";
import Sidenav from "./layout/sidenav/sidenav";
import { useState } from "react";
import Footer from "./layout/footer/footer";
import Home from "./pages/home/home";

function App() {
  const [opened, setOpened] = useState(false);

  return (
    <div>
      <BrowserRouter>
        <TopBar opened={opened}
setOpened={setOpened} />
        <Sidenav opened={opened}
setOpened={setOpened} />
        <main className="main">
```

```
        <Routes>
          <Route path="/" element={<Home />} />
          <Route path="/home" element={<Home />} />
        </Routes>
      </main>
      <Footer />
    </BrowserRouter>
  </div>
  );
}

export default App;
```

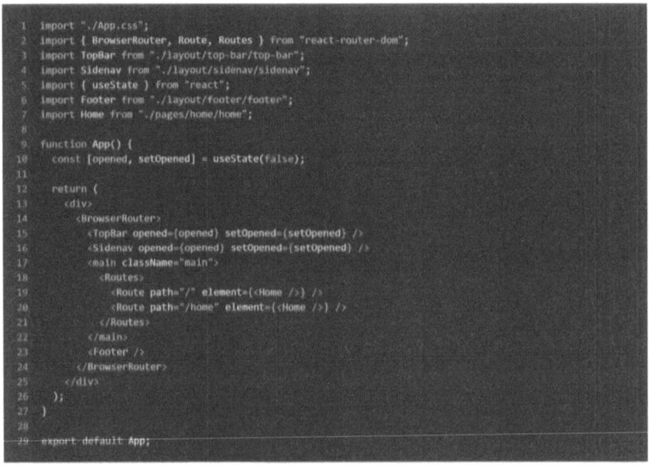

```jsx
1   import "./App.css";
2   import { BrowserRouter, Route, Routes } from "react-router-dom";
3   import TopBar from "./layout/top-bar/top-bar";
4   import Sidenav from "./layout/sidenav/sidenav";
5   import { useState } from "react";
6   import Footer from "./layout/footer/footer";
7   import Home from "./pages/home/home";
8
9   function App() {
10    const [opened, setOpened] = useState(false);
11
12    return (
13      <div>
14        <BrowserRouter>
15          <TopBar opened={opened} setOpened={setOpened} />
16          <Sidenav opened={opened} setOpened={setOpened} />
17          <main className="main">
18            <Routes>
19              <Route path="/" element={<Home />} />
20              <Route path="/home" element={<Home />} />
21            </Routes>
22          </main>
23          <Footer />
24        </BrowserRouter>
25      </div>
26    );
27  }
28
29  export default App;
```

Chapter 9: [Home] Promotion Component

9.1 Preview

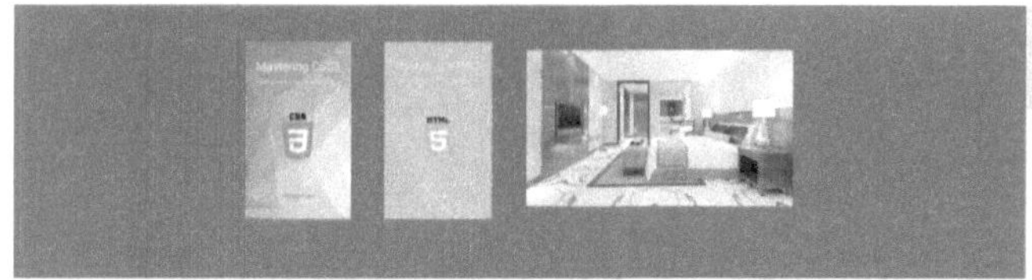

9.2 Create It

- Create a new folder "promotion" inside "pages/home/components"

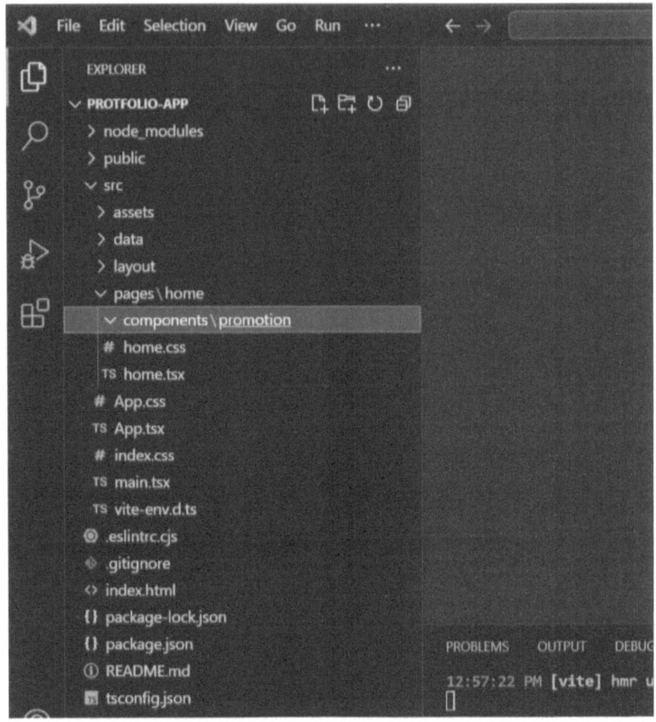

- Create promotion.tsx
- Create promotion.css

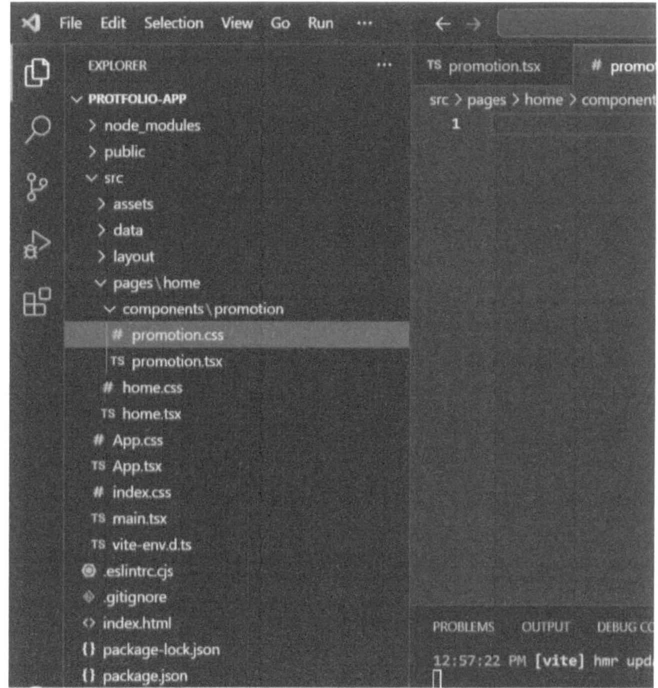

9.3 TSX

```tsx
import "./promotion.css";

function Promotion() {
  return (
    <section className="promotion">
      <img

src="images/promotion/book-mastering-css3.jpg"
        alt=""
```

```jsx
        title="Mastering CSS3 A Comprehensive
Guide to Modern Web Styling"
        className="book link"
      />
      <img

src="images/promotion/book-mastering-html5.jpg"
        alt=""
        title="Mastering HTML5: The Complete
Guide to Modern Web Development"
        className="book link"
      />
      <img

src="images/promotion/course-hotel-booking-app.
jpg"
        alt=""
        title="Creative CSS Projects: Hotel
Booking App"
        className="course link"
      />
    </section>
  );
}
export default Promotion;
```

```jsx
import "./promotion.css";

function Promotion() {
  return (
    <section className="promotion">
      <img
        src="images/promotion/book-mastering-css3.jpg"
        alt=""
        title="Mastering CSS3 A Comprehensive Guide to Modern Web Styling"
        className="book link"
      />
      <img
        src="images/promotion/book-mastering-html5.jpg"
        alt=""
        title="Mastering HTML5: The Complete Guide to Modern Web Development"
        className="book link"
      />
      <img
        src="images/promotion/course-hotel-booking-app.jpg"
        alt=""
        title="Creative CSS Projects: Hotel Booking App"
        className="course link"
      />
    </section>
  );
}
export default Promotion;
```

9.4 CSS

```css
.promotion {
  display: flex;
  justify-content: center;
  align-items: center;
  padding: 40px 20px;
  @media (min-width: 760px) {
    gap: 50px;
    padding: 40px 20px;
  }
}
.book {
  width: 160px;
  height: auto;
  max-height: 100%;
  cursor: pointer;
  display: none;
  @media (min-width: 760px) {
    display: block;
```

```css
  }
}
.course {
  max-width: 100%;
  height: auto;
  max-height: 100%;
  cursor: pointer;
  @media (min-width: 760px) {
    width: 400px;
  }
}
```

```css
1   .promotion {
2     display: flex;
3     justify-content: center;
4     align-items: center;
5     padding: 40px 20px;
6     @media (min-width: 760px) {
7       gap: 50px;
8       padding: 40px 20px;
9     }
10  }
11  .book {
12    width: 160px;
13    height: auto;
14    max-height: 100%;
15    cursor: pointer;
16    display: none;
17    @media (min-width: 760px) {
18      display: block;
19    }
20  }
21  .course {
22    max-width: 100%;
23    height: auto;
24    max-height: 100%;
25    cursor: pointer;
26    @media (min-width: 760px) {
27      width: 400px;
28    }
29  }
30
```

9.5 Use It

Use it in home.tsx

```tsx
import Promotion from
"./components/promotion/promotion";
```

```
function Home() {
  return (
    <>
      <Promotion />
    </>
  );
}

export default Home;
```

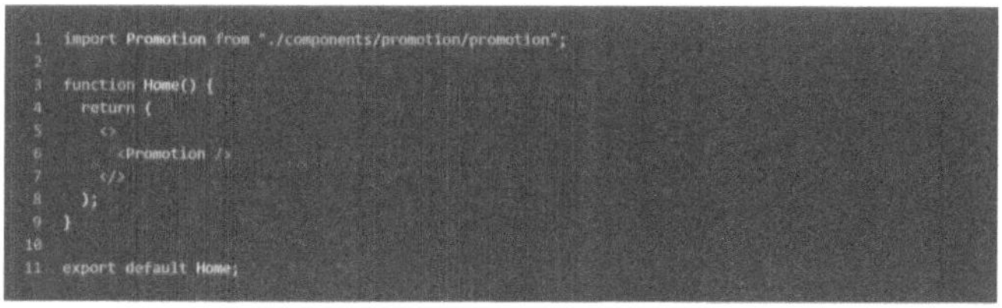

```
1   import Promotion from "./components/promotion/promotion";
2
3   function Home() {
4     return (
5       <>
6         <Promotion />
7       </>
8     );
9   }
10
11  export default Home;
```

Chapter 10: [Home] Welcome Component

10.1 Preview

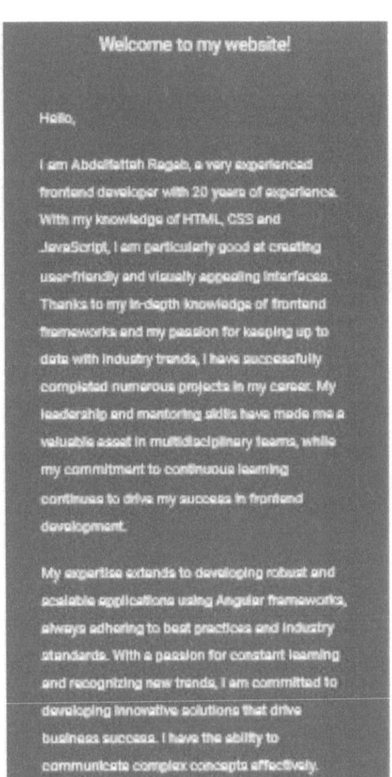

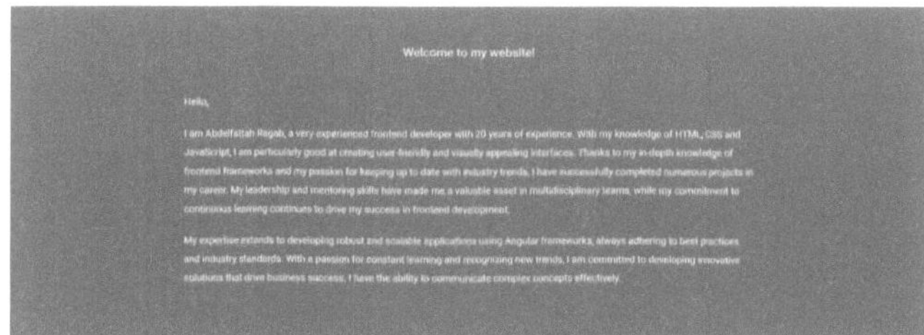

10.2 Create It

- Create a new folder "welcome" inside "pages/home/components"

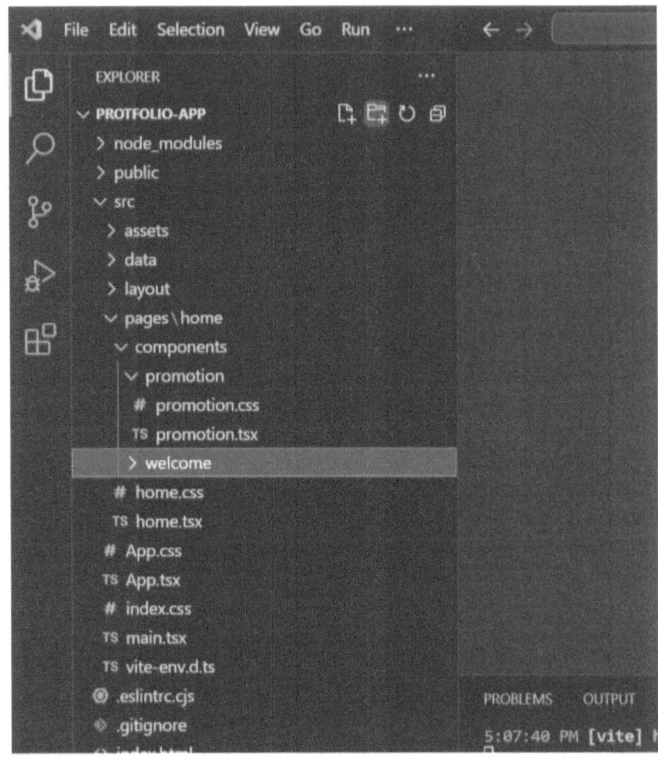

- Create welcome.tsx
- Create welcome.css

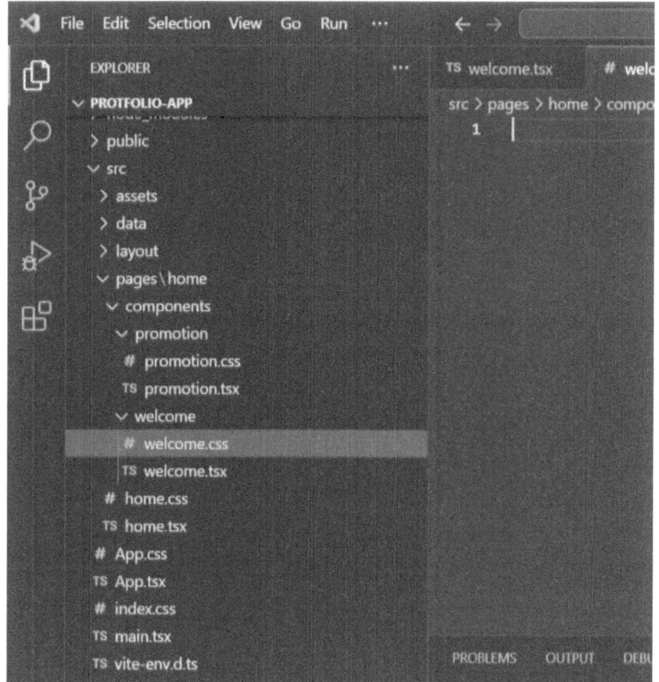

10.3 TSX

```tsx
import "./welcome.css";

function Welcome() {
  return (
    <section className="welcome">
      <header
className="welcome-header">Welcome to my
website!</header>
      <div className="welcome-content">
        <p>Hello,</p>
```

<p>
I am Abdelfattah Ragab, a very experienced frontend developer with 20 years of experience. With my knowledge of HTML, CSS and JavaScript, I am particularly good at creating user-friendly and visually appealing interfaces. Thanks to my in-depth knowledge of frontend frameworks and my passion for keeping up to date with industry trends, I have successfully completed numerous projects in my career. My leadership and mentoring skills have made me a valuable asset in multidisciplinary teams, while my commitment to continuous learning continues to drive my success in frontend development.
</p>
<p>
My expertise extends to developing robust and scalable applications using Angular frameworks, always adhering to best practices and industry standards. With a passion for constant learning and recognizing new trends, I am committed to developing innovative solutions that drive business success. I have the ability to communicate complex concepts effectively.
</p>

```jsx
      </div>
    </section>
  );
}

export default Welcome;
```

```jsx
1   import "./welcome.css";
2
3   function Welcome() {
4     return (
5       <section className="welcome">
6         <header className="welcome-header">Welcome to my website!</header>
7         <div className="welcome-content">
8           <p>Hello,</p>
9           <p>
10            I am Abdelfattah Ragab, a very experienced frontend developer with 20
11            years of experience. With my knowledge of HTML, CSS and JavaScript, I
12            am particularly good at creating user-friendly and visually appealing
13            interfaces. Thanks to my in-depth knowledge of frontend frameworks and
14            my passion for keeping up to date with industry trends, I have
15            successfully completed numerous projects in my career. My leadership
16            and mentoring skills have made me a valuable asset in
17            multidisciplinary teams, while my commitment to continuous learning
18            continues to drive my success in frontend development.
19          </p>
20          <p>
21            My expertise extends to developing robust and scalable applications
22            using Angular frameworks, always adhering to best practices and
23            industry standards. With a passion for constant learning and
24            recognizing new trends, I am committed to developing innovative
25            solutions that drive business success. I have the ability to
26            communicate complex concepts effectively.
27          </p>
28        </div>
29      </section>
30    );
31  }
32
33  export default Welcome;
```

10.4 CSS

```css
.welcome {
  padding: 100px 20px;
  line-height: 30px;
  cursor: default;
}
.welcome-header {
  text-align: center;
  font-size: 20px;
```

```css
  margin-bottom: 40px;
}
.welcome-content p {
  padding: 10px 0px;
}
```

```css
1   .welcome {
2       padding: 100px 20px;
3       line-height: 30px;
4       cursor: default;
5   }
6   .welcome-header {
7       text-align: center;
8       font-size: 20px;
9       margin-bottom: 40px;
10  }
11  .welcome-content p {
12      padding: 10px 0px;
13  }
14
```

10.5 Use It

Use it in home.tsx

```tsx
import Promotion from
"./components/promotion/promotion";
import Welcome from
"./components/welcome/welcome";

function Home() {
  return (
    <>
      <Promotion />
      <Welcome />
    </>
  );
}

export default Home;
```

```jsx
import Promotion from "./components/promotion/promotion";
import Welcome from "./components/welcome/welcome";

function Home() {
  return (
    <>
      <Promotion />
      <Welcome />
    </>
  );
}

export default Home;
```

Chapter 11: [Home] Badges Component

11.1 Preview

11.2 Create It

- Create a new folder "badges" inside "pages/home/components"

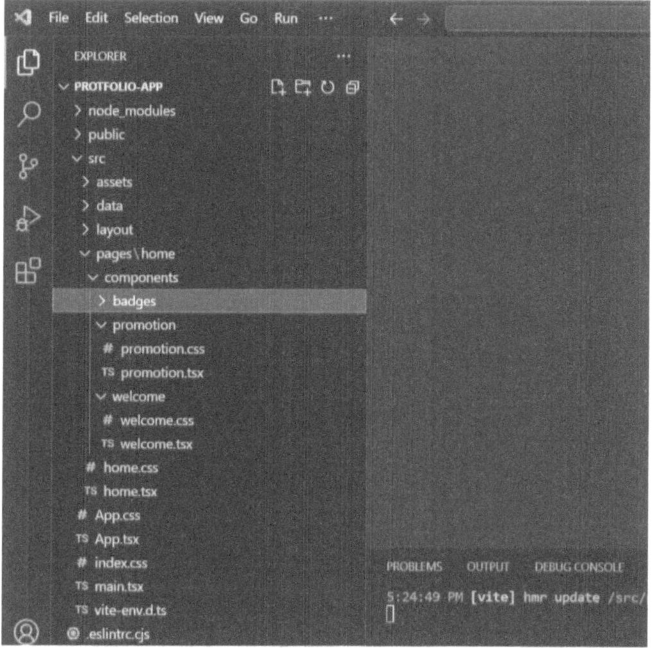

- Create badges.tsx
- Create badges.css

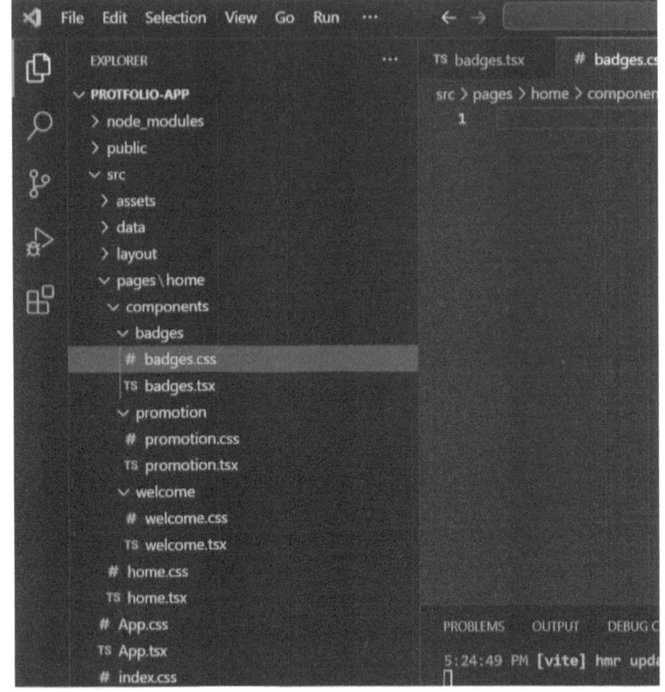

11.3 TSX

```tsx
import "./badges.css";

function Badges() {
  return (
    <section className="badges">
      <img
        src="images/badges/angular.png"
        alt=""
        title="Expert Angular Developer -
Certified Level 3"
```

```jsx
          className="badge link"
        />
        <img
          src="images/badges/oracle.png"
          alt=""
          title="Oracle Certified Professional:
Java SE 11 Developer"
          className="badge link"
        />
        <img
          src="images/badges/google.png"
          alt=""
          title="Google Cloud Certified
Professional Cloud Architect"
          className="badge link"
        />
        <img
          src="images/badges/aws.png"
          alt=""
          title="AWS Certified Solutions
Architect Associate"
          className="badge link"
        />
    </section>
  );
}

export default Badges;
```

```jsx
 1  import "./badges.css";
 2
 3  function Badges() {
 4    return (
 5      <section className="badges">
 6        <img
 7          src="images/badges/angular.png"
 8          alt=""
 9          title="Expert Angular Developer - Certified Level 3"
10          className="badge link"
11        />
12        <img
13          src="images/badges/oracle.png"
14          alt=""
15          title="Oracle Certified Professional: Java SE 11 Developer"
16          className="badge link"
17        />
18        <img
19          src="images/badges/google.png"
20          alt=""
21          title="Google Cloud Certified Professional Cloud Architect"
22          className="badge link"
23        />
24        <img
25          src="images/badges/aws.png"
26          alt=""
27          title="AWS Certified Solutions Architect Associate"
28          className="badge link"
29        />
30      </section>
31    );
32  }
33
34  export default Badges;
```

11.4 CSS

```css
.badges {
  display: grid;
  grid-template-columns: 1fr 1fr;
  place-items: center center;
  column-gap: 0px;
  row-gap: 80px;
  padding: 60px 0px;
  @media (min-width: 760px) {
    display: flex;
    justify-content: center;
    align-items: center;
    gap: 80px;
  }
}
```

```css
.badges .badge {
  max-width: 80px;
  max-height: 80px;
  width: auto;
  height: auto;
  cursor: pointer;
  opacity: 0.9;
  @media (min-width: 760px) {
    max-width: 100px;
    max-height: 100px;
  }
}
```

```html
1   <section class="welcome">
2     <header class="welcome-header">Welcome to my website!</header>
3     <div class="welcome-content">
4       <p>Hello,</p>
5       <p>
6         I am Abdelfattah Ragab, a very experienced frontend developer with 20
7         years of experience. With my knowledge of HTML, CSS and JavaScript, I am
8         particularly good at creating user-friendly and visually appealing
9         interfaces. Thanks to my in-depth knowledge of frontend frameworks and my
10        passion for keeping up to date with industry trends, I have successfully
11        completed numerous projects in my career. My leadership and mentoring
12        skills have made me a valuable asset in multidisciplinary teams, while my
13        commitment to continuous learning continues to drive my success in
14        frontend development.
15      </p>
16      <p>
17        My expertise extends to developing robust and scalable applications using
18        Angular frameworks, always adhering to best practices and industry
19        standards. With a passion for constant learning and recognizing new
20        trends, I am committed to developing innovative solutions that drive
21        business success. I have the ability to communicate complex concepts
22        effectively.
23      </p>
24    </div>
25  </section>
26
```

11.5 Use It

Use it in home.tsx

```tsx
import Badges from
"./components/badges/badges";
import Promotion from
"./components/promotion/promotion";
```

```jsx
import Welcome from
"./components/welcome/welcome";

function Home() {
  return (
    <>
      <Promotion />
      <Welcome />
      <Badges />
    </>
  );
}

export default Home;
```

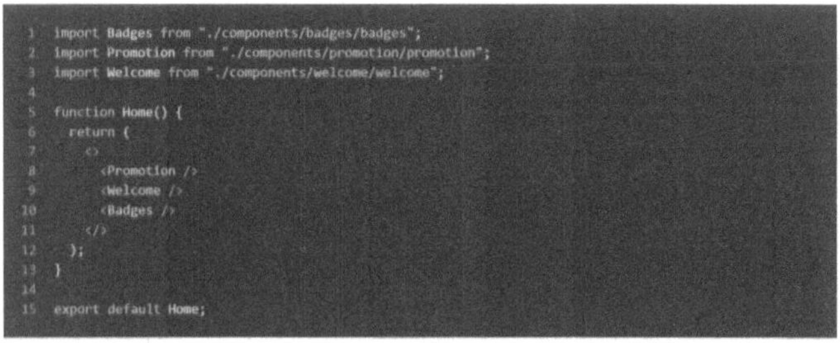

```jsx
1  import Badges from "./components/badges/badges";
2  import Promotion from "./components/promotion/promotion";
3  import Welcome from "./components/welcome/welcome";
4
5  function Home() {
6    return (
7      <>
8        <Promotion />
9        <Welcome />
10       <Badges />
11     </>
12   );
13 }
14
15 export default Home;
```

Chapter 12: About Page

12.1 Preview

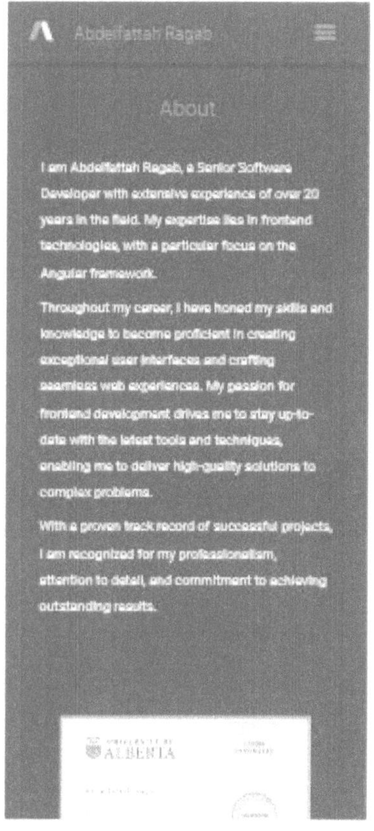

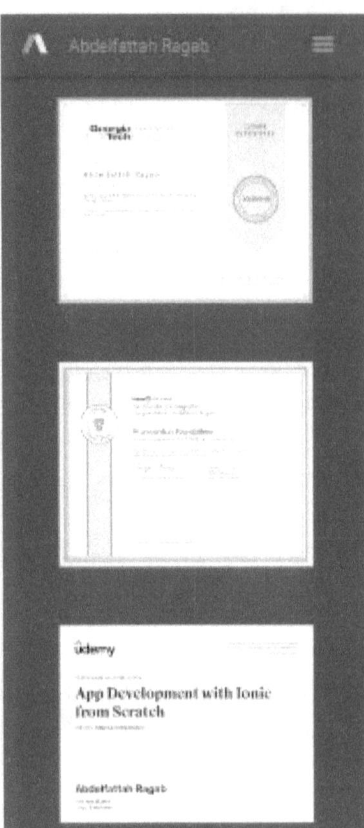
Georgia
Tech
Abdelfattah Ragab

udemy
App Development with Ionic
from Scratch
Abdelfattah Ragab

Abdelfattah Ragab
aws CERTIFIED
Abdelfattah Ragab
AWS Certified Solutions Architect - Associate

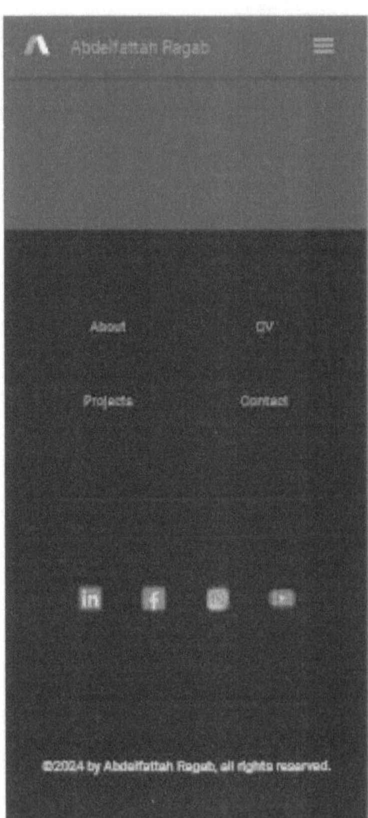

Abdelfattah Ragab
About
CV
Projects
Contact
©2024 by Abdelfattah Ragab, all rights reserved.

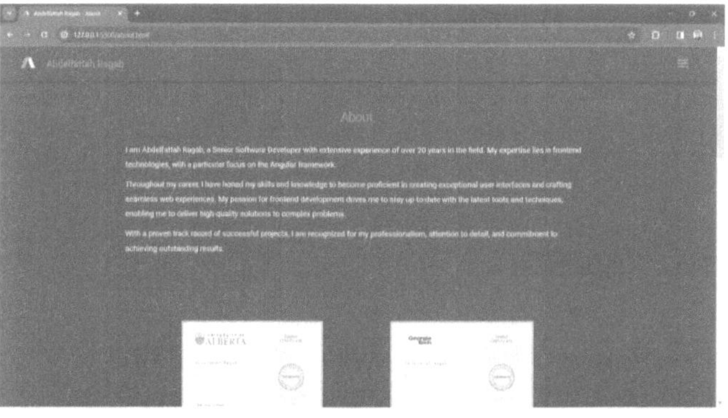

Abdelfattah Ragab
About
I am Abdelfattah Ragab, a Senior Software Developer with extensive experience of over 20 years in the field. My expertise lies in frontend technologies, with a particular focus on the Angular framework.
Throughout my career, I have honed my skills and knowledge to become proficient in creating exceptional user interfaces and crafting seamless web experiences. My passion for frontend development drives me to stay up-to-date with the latest tools and techniques, enabling me to deliver high-quality solutions to complex problems.
With a proven track record of successful projects, I am recognized for my professionalism, attention to detail, and commitment to achieving outstanding results.

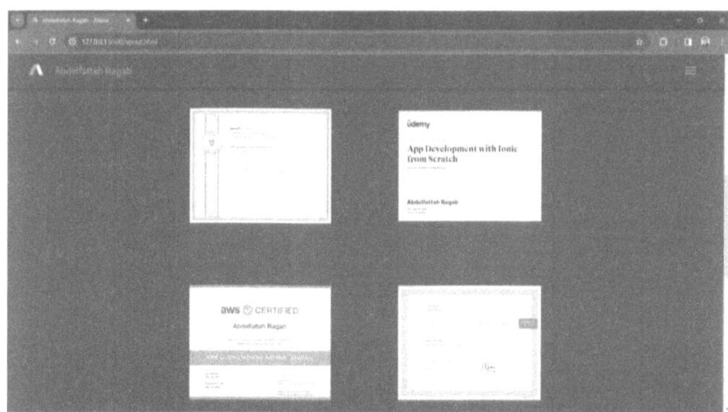

Abdelfattah Ragab
Udemy
App Development with Ionic from Scratch
Abdelfattah Ragab
aws CERTIFIED
Abdelfattah Ragab

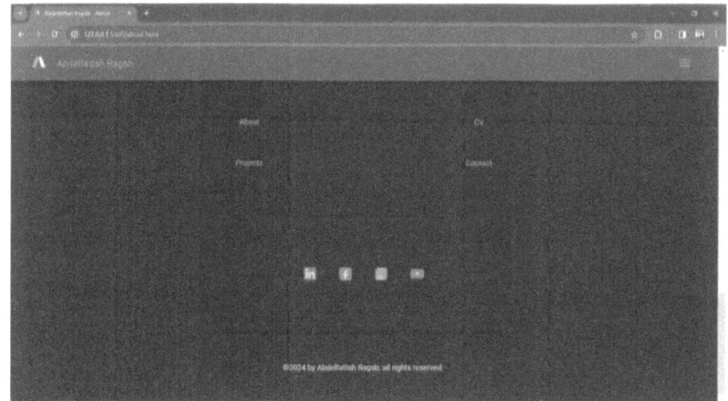

Abdelfattah Ragab
About
CV
Projects
Connect
©2024 by Abdelfattah Ragab, all rights reserved.

12.2 Page Outline

```
<Bio />
<Certificates />
```

12.3 Create It

- Create a new folder "about" inside "pages"

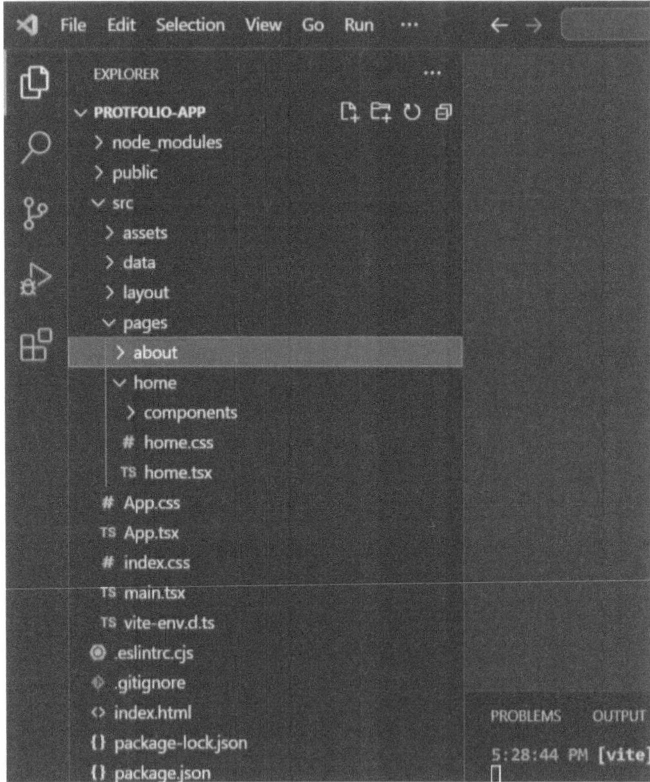

- Create about.tsx

- Create about.css

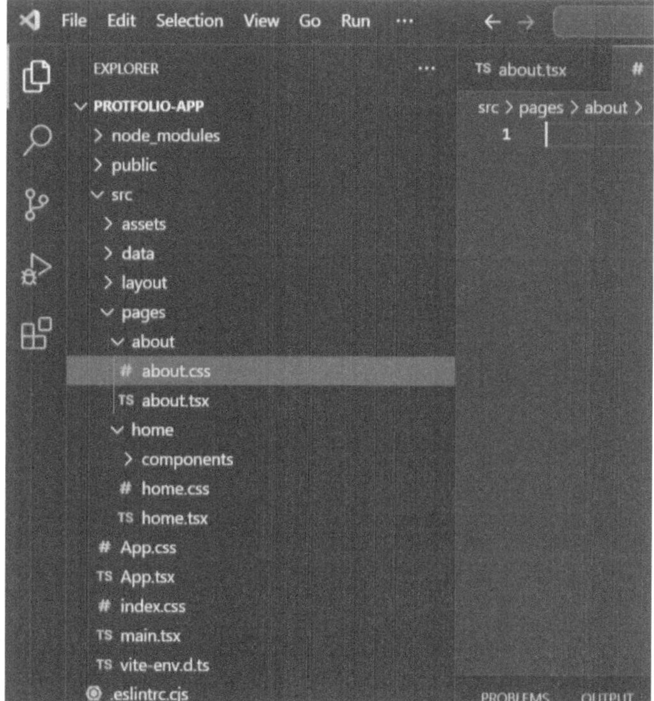

12.4 TSX

```
function About() {
  return <></>;
}


export default About;
```

12.5 CSS

Nothing

12.6 Set Title

```
function About() {
  return (
    <>
      <header
className="main-title">About</header>
    </>
  );
}


export default About;
```

```
function About() {
  return (
    <>
      <header className="main-title">About</header>
    </>
  );
}

export default About;
```

12.7 Add Route

Add new route to App.tsx as follows

```
import "./App.css";
import { BrowserRouter, Route, Routes } from
"react-router-dom";
import TopBar from "./layout/top-bar/top-bar";
import Sidenav from "./layout/sidenav/sidenav";
import { useState } from "react";
```

```jsx
import Footer from "./layout/footer/footer";
import Home from "./pages/home/home";
import About from "./pages/about/about";

function App() {
  const [opened, setOpened] = useState(false);

  return (
    <div>
      <BrowserRouter>
        <TopBar opened={opened} setOpened={setOpened} />
        <Sidenav opened={opened} setOpened={setOpened} />
        <main className="main">
          <Routes>
            <Route path="/" element={<Home />} />
            <Route path="/home" element={<Home />} />
            <Route path="/about" element={<About />} />
          </Routes>
        </main>
        <Footer />
      </BrowserRouter>
    </div>
  );
}

export default App;
```

```jsx
import "./App.css";
import { BrowserRouter, Route, Routes } from "react-router-dom";
import TopBar from "./layout/top-bar/top-bar";
import Sidenav from "./layout/sidenav/sidenav";
import { useState } from "react";
import Footer from "./layout/footer/footer";
import Home from "./pages/home/home";
import About from "./pages/about/about";

function App() {
  const [opened, setOpened] = useState(false);

  return (
    <div>
      <BrowserRouter>
        <TopBar opened={opened} setOpened={setOpened} />
        <Sidenav opened={opened} setOpened={setOpened} />
        <main className="main">
          <Routes>
            <Route path="/" element={<Home />} />
            <Route path="/home" element={<Home />} />
            <Route path="/about" element={<About />} />
          </Routes>
        </main>
        <Footer />
      </BrowserRouter>
    </div>
  );
}

export default App;
```

Chapter 13: [About] Bio Component

13.1 Preview

I am Abdelfattah Ragab, a Senior Software Developer with extensive experience of over 20 years in the field. My expertise lies in frontend technologies, with a particular focus on the Angular framework.

Throughout my career, I have honed my skills and knowledge to become proficient in creating exceptional user interfaces and crafting seamless web experiences. My passion for frontend development drives me to stay up-to-date with the latest tools and techniques, enabling me to deliver high-quality solutions to complex problems.

With a proven track record of successful projects, I am recognized for my professionalism, attention to detail, and commitment to achieving outstanding results.

I am Abdelfattah Ragab, a Senior Software Developer with extensive experience of over 20 years in the field. My expertise lies in frontend technologies, with a particular focus on the Angular framework.

Throughout my career, I have honed my skills and knowledge to become proficient in creating exceptional user interfaces and crafting seamless web experiences. My passion for frontend development drives me to stay up-to-date with the latest tools and techniques, enabling me to deliver high-quality solutions to complex problems.

With a proven track record of successful projects, I am recognized for my professionalism, attention to detail, and commitment to achieving outstanding results.

13.2 Create It

- Create a new folder "bio" inside
  "pages/about/components"

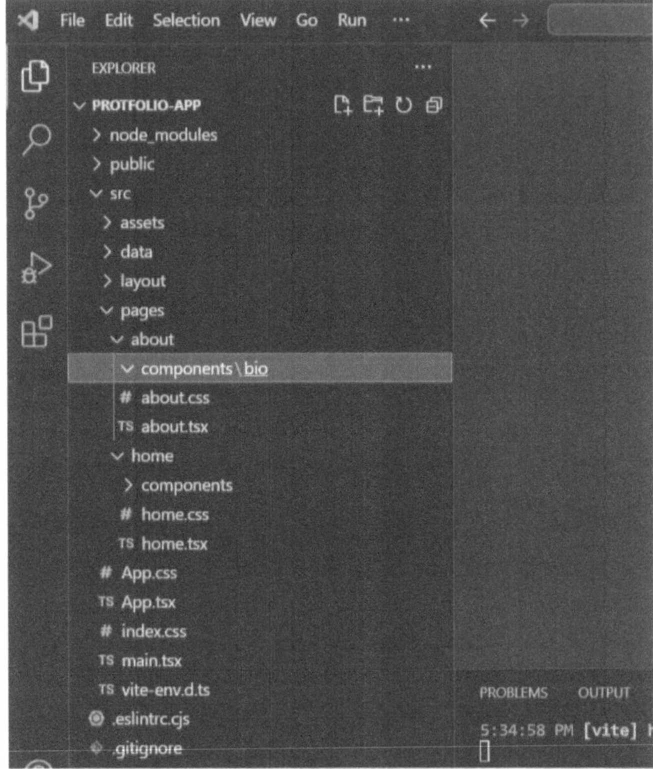

- Create bio.tsx
- Create bio.css

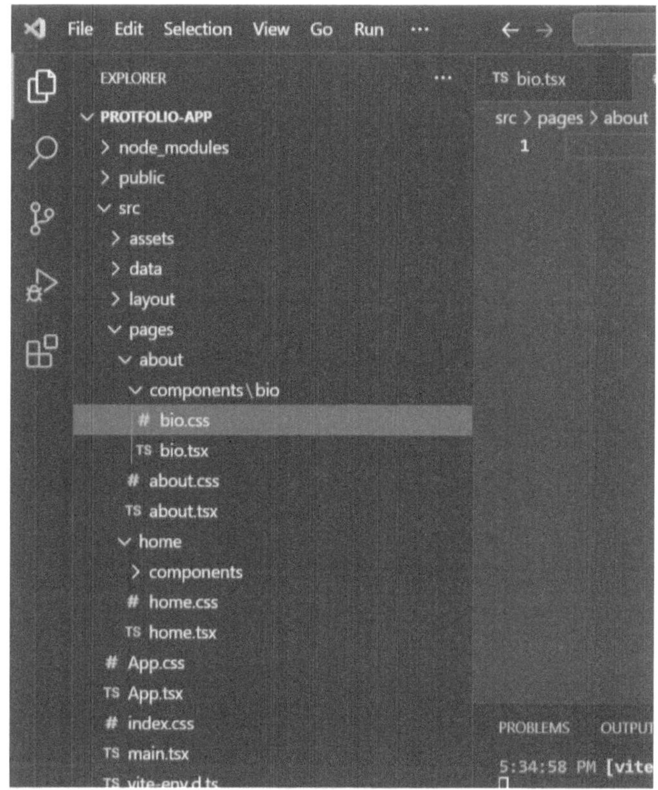

13.3 TSX

```tsx
import "./bio.css";

function Bio() {
  return (
    <section className="bio">
      <p>
```

```jsx
        I am Abdelfattah Ragab, a Senior
Software Developer with extensive
        experience of over 20 years in the
field. My expertise lies in frontend
        technologies, with a particular focus
on the Angular framework.
      </p>
      <p>
        Throughout my career, I have honed my
skills and knowledge to become
        proficient in creating exceptional user
interfaces and crafting seamless
        web experiences. My passion for
frontend development drives me to stay
        up-to-date with the latest tools and
techniques, enabling me to deliver
        high-quality solutions to complex
problems.
      </p>
      <p>
        With a proven track record of
successful projects, I am recognized for
        my professionalism, attention to
detail, and commitment to achieving
        outstanding results.
      </p>
    </section>
  );
}

export default Bio;
```

```
 1  import "./bio.css";
 2
 3  function Bio() {
 4    return (
 5      <section className="bio">
 6        <p>
 7          I am Abdelfattah Ragab, a Senior Software Developer with extensive
 8          experience of over 20 years in the field. My expertise lies in frontend
 9          technologies, with a particular focus on the Angular framework.
10        </p>
11        <p>
12          Throughout my career, I have honed my skills and knowledge to become
13          proficient in creating exceptional user interfaces and crafting seamless
14          web experiences. My passion for frontend development drives me to stay
15          up-to-date with the latest tools and techniques, enabling me to deliver
16          high-quality solutions to complex problems.
17        </p>
18        <p>
19          With a proven track record of successful projects, I am recognized for
20          my professionalism, attention to detail, and commitment to achieving
21          outstanding results.
22        </p>
23      </section>
24    );
25  }
26
27  export default Bio;
```

13.4 CSS

```css
.bio p {
  margin: 10px 0px;
  line-height: 26px;
}
```

```
1  .bio p {
2    margin: 10px 0px;
3    line-height: 26px;
4  }
```

13.5 Use It

Use it in the page

```
import Bio from "./bio/bio";
```

```
function About() {
```

```jsx
  return (
    <>
      <header className="main-title">About</header>
      <Bio />
    </>
  );
}

export default About;
```

```jsx
1   import Bio from "./bio/bio";
2
3   function About() {
4     return (
5       <>
6         <header className="main-title">About</header>
7         <Bio />
8       </>
9     );
10  }
11
12  export default About;
```

Chapter 14: Certificates Data

14.1 Create It

Create certificates.data.ts in the "data" folder

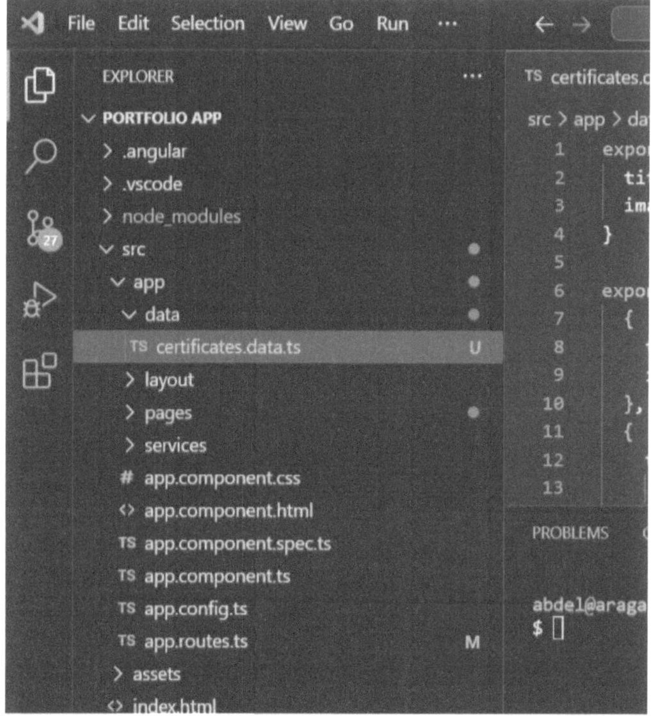

14.2 TS

```
export interface Certificate {
  title: string;
```

```typescript
  imageUrl: string;
}

export const CERTIFICATES: Certificate[] = [
  {
    title: 'Software Design and Architecture -
University of Alberta',
    imageUrl:
'assets/images/certificates/architecture.png',
  },
  {
    title:
      'Improve Your English Communication
Skills - Georgia Institute of Technology',
    imageUrl:
'assets/images/certificates/english.png',
  },
  {
    title: 'Microservices Foundations -
LinkedIn',
    imageUrl:
'assets/images/certificates/microservices.png',
  },
  {
    title: 'Ionic - Udemy',
    imageUrl:
'assets/images/certificates/ionic.png',
  },
  {
    title: 'AWS Certified Solutions Architect -
Associate',
    imageUrl:
'assets/images/certificates/aws.png',
  },
```

```typescript
  {
    title: 'Oracle Certified Professional, Java SE 11 Programmer',
    imageUrl: 'assets/images/certificates/java-2.png',
  },
];
```

```typescript
export interface Certificate {
  title: string;
  imageUrl: string;
}

export const CERTIFICATES: Certificate[] = [
  {
    title: 'Software Design and Architecture - University of Alberta',
    imageUrl: 'assets/images/certificates/architecture.png',
  },
  {
    title:
      'Improve Your English Communication Skills - Georgia Institute of Technology',
    imageUrl: 'assets/images/certificates/english.png',
  },
  {
    title: 'Microservices Foundations - LinkedIn',
    imageUrl: 'assets/images/certificates/microservices.png',
  },
  {
    title: 'Ionic - Udemy',
    imageUrl: 'assets/images/certificates/ionic.png',
  },
  {
    title: 'AWS Certified Solutions Architect - Associate',
    imageUrl: 'assets/images/certificates/aws.png',
  },
  {
    title: 'Oracle Certified Professional, Java SE 11 Programmer',
    imageUrl: 'assets/images/certificates/java-2.png',
  },
];
```

Chapter 15: [About] Certificates Component

15.1 Preview

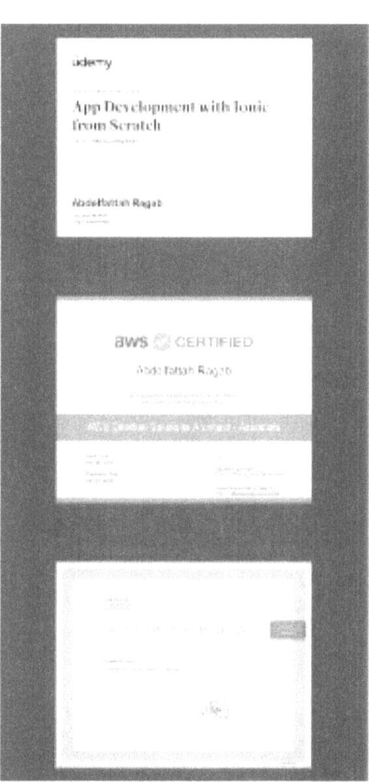
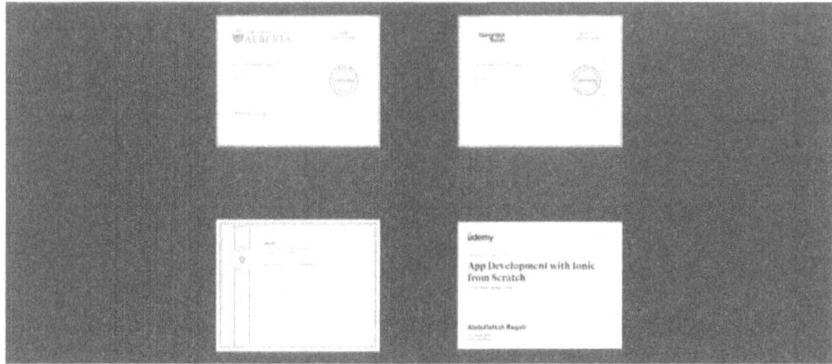

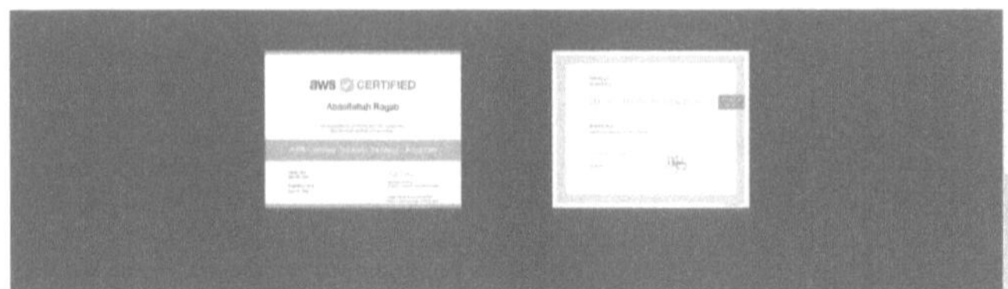

15.2 Create It

- Create a new folder "certificates" inside the
  "pages/about/components" folder

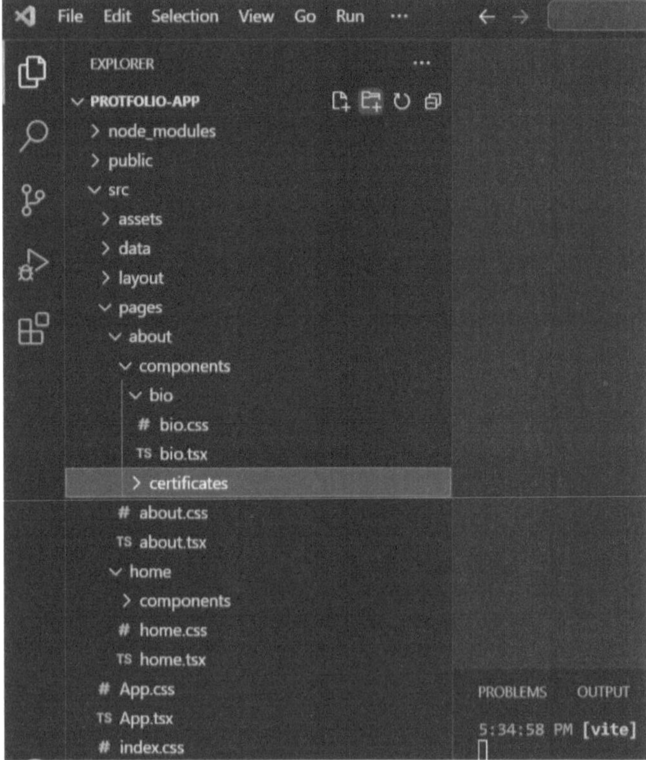

- Create certificates.tsx
- Create certificates.css

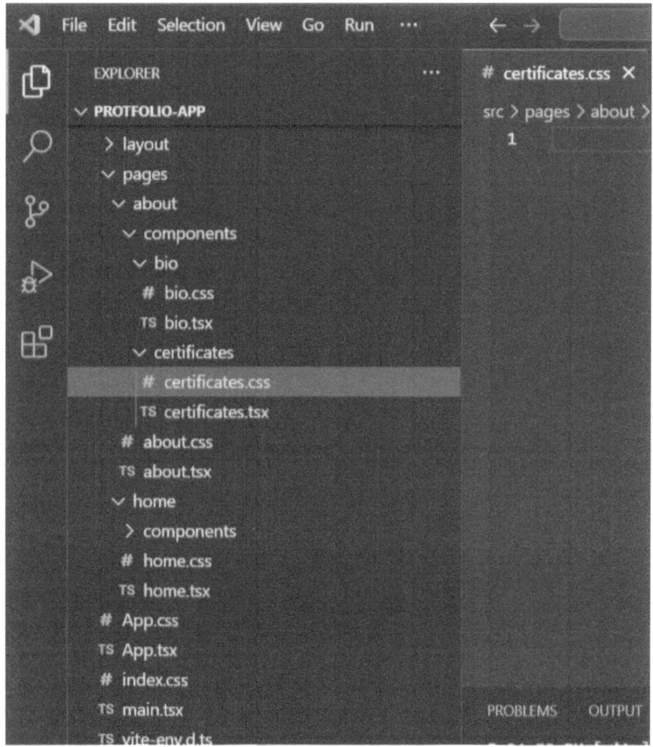

15.3 TSX

```tsx
import { Certificate, CERTIFICATES } from
"../../../../data/certificates.data";
import "./certificates.css";

function Certificates() {
```

```
  const createCertificateElement =
(certificate: Certificate) => (
    <img
      key={certificate.title}
      src={certificate.imageUrl}
      alt={certificate.title}
      title={certificate.title}
      className="certificate link"
    />
  );
  return (
    <section className="certificates">

{CERTIFICATES.map(createCertificateElement)}
    </section>
  );
}


export default Certificates;
```

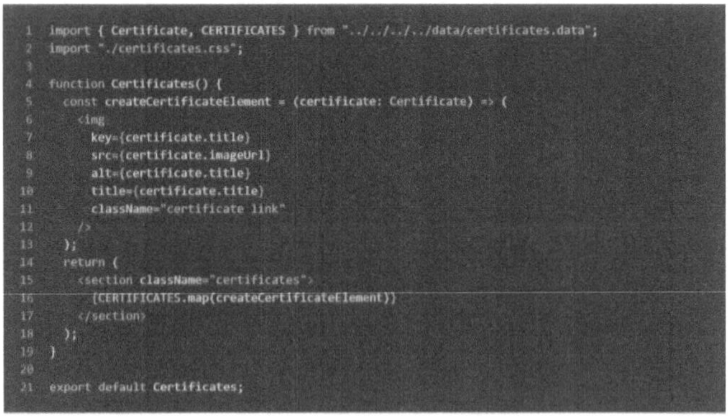

```
1   import { Certificate, CERTIFICATES } from "../../../../data/certificates.data";
2   import "./certificates.css";
3
4   function Certificates() {
5     const createCertificateElement = (certificate: Certificate) => (
6       <img
7         key={certificate.title}
8         src={certificate.imageUrl}
9         alt={certificate.title}
10        title={certificate.title}
11        className="certificate link"
12      />
13    );
14    return (
15      <section className="certificates">
16        {CERTIFICATES.map(createCertificateElement)}
17      </section>
18    );
19  }
20
21  export default Certificates;
```

15.4 CSS

```css
.certificates {
  display: grid;
  grid-template-columns: 1fr;
  place-items: center center;
  padding: 100px 20px;
  column-gap: 20px;
  row-gap: 60px;
  @media (min-width: 760px) {
    padding: 120px 60px;
    grid-template-columns: 1fr 1fr;
    row-gap: 120px;
  }
}
.certificate {
  width: 300px;
  height: auto;
}
```

```css
1  .certificates {
2    display: grid;
3    grid-template-columns: 1fr;
4    place-items: center center;
5    padding: 100px 20px;
6    column-gap: 20px;
7    row-gap: 60px;
8    @media (min-width: 760px) {
9      padding: 120px 60px;
10     grid-template-columns: 1fr 1fr;
11     row-gap: 120px;
12   }
13 }
14 .certificate {
15   width: 300px;
16   height: auto;
17 }
```

15.5 Use It

Use it in about.tsx

```jsx
import Bio from "./components/bio/bio";
import Certificates from
"./components/certificates/certificates";

function About() {
  return (
    <>
      <header
className="main-title">About</header>
      <Bio />
      <Certificates />
    </>
  );
}

export default About;
```

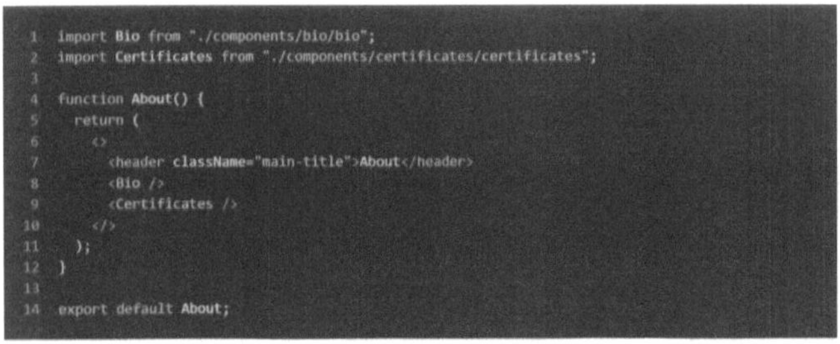

```jsx
1   import Bio from "./components/bio/bio";
2   import Certificates from "./components/certificates/certificates";
3
4   function About() {
5     return (
6       <>
7         <header className="main-title">About</header>
8         <Bio />
9         <Certificates />
10      </>
11    );
12  }
13
14  export default About;
```

Chapter 16: CV Page

16.1 Preview

- Optimize the complex SQL queries

- Create PDF and Word reports

Senior Software Developer - .NET/Angular

2014 - 2017

Work for clients online:

- Develop the backend system using .NET

- Develop the client side part with Angular

- Search engine optimization

- Copywriting, advertising and marketing

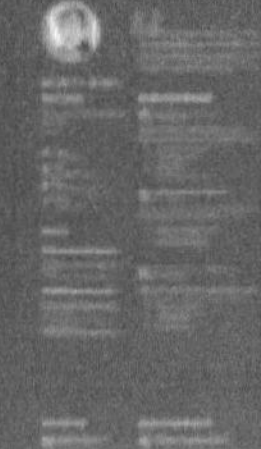

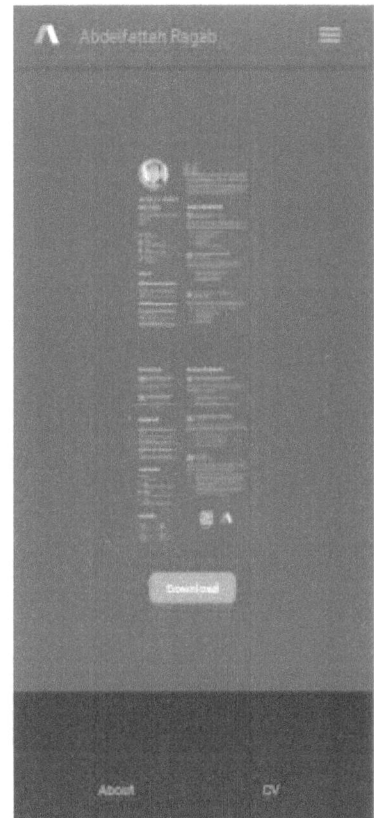

Abdelfattah Ragab
Download
About
CV

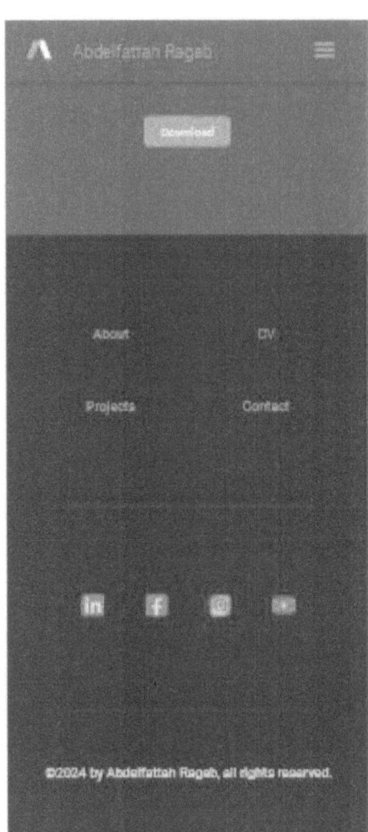
Abdelfattah Ragab
Download
About
CV
Projects
Contact

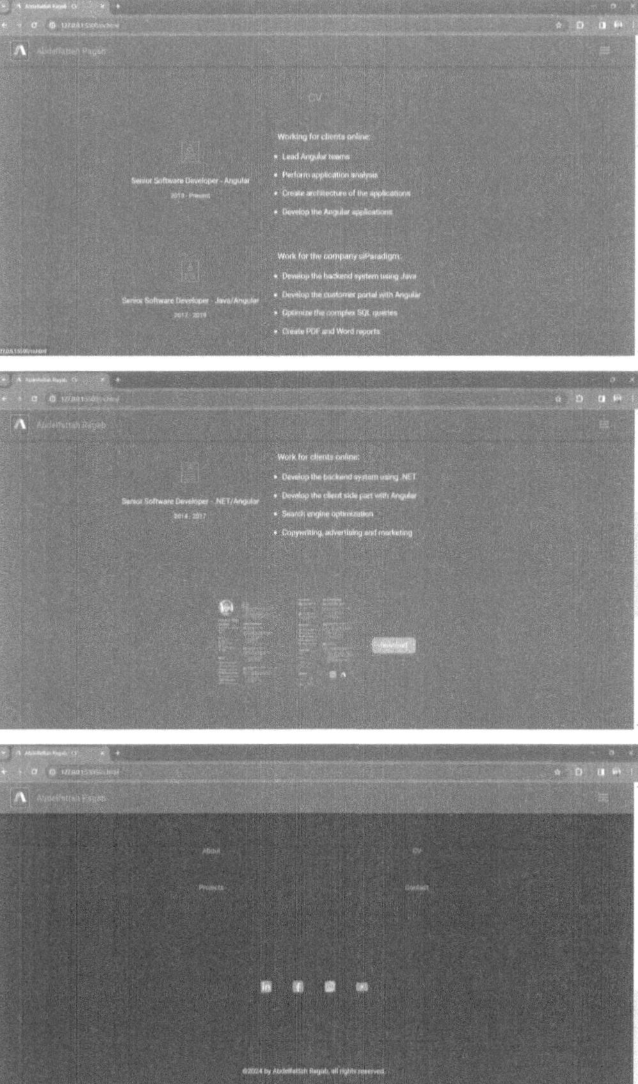

Abdelfattah Ragab
CV

Senior Software Developer - Angular
2019 - Present

Working for clients online:
Lead Angular teams
Perform application analysis
Create architecture of the applications
Develop the Angular applications

Senior Software Developer - Java/Angular
2017 - 2019

Work for the company siParadigm:
Develop the backend system using Java
Develop the customer portal with Angular
Optimize the complex SQL queries
Create PDF and Word reports

Senior Software Developer - .NET/Angular
2014 - 2017

Work for clients online:
Develop the backend system using .NET
Develop the client side part with Angular
Search engine optimization
Copywriting, advertising and marketing

About
CV
Projects
Contact

©2024 by Abdelfattah Ragab, all rights reserved.

16.2 Page Outline

```
<Experiences />
<DownloadCV />
```

16.3 Create It

- Create a new folder "cv" inside "pages"

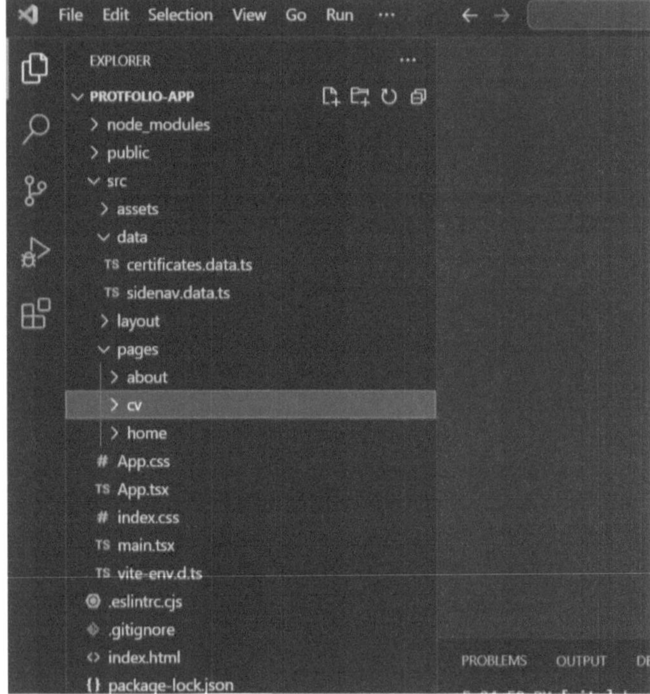

- Create cv.tsx
- Create cv.css

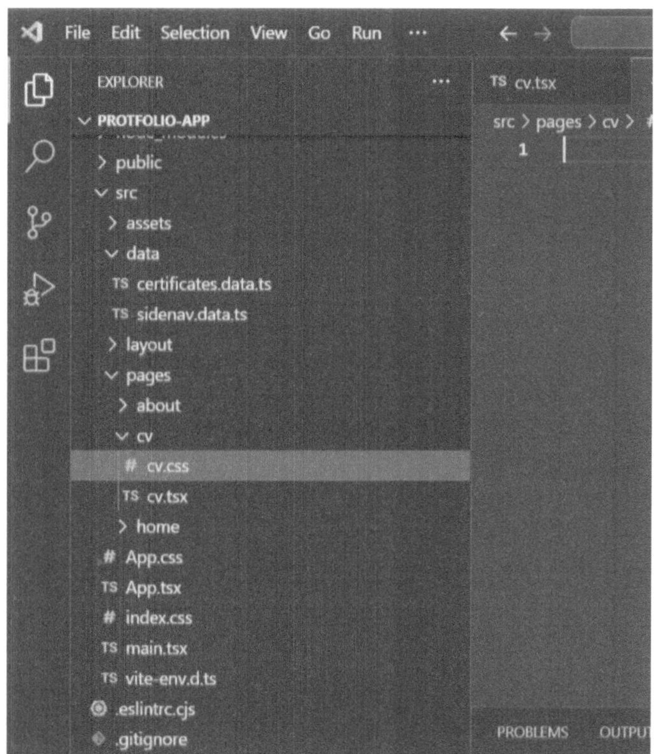

16.4 TSX

```tsx
function CV() {
  return <></>;
}

export default CV;
```

```
1  function CV() {
2    return <></>;
3  }
4
5  export default CV;
```

16.5 Set Title

```
function CV() {
  return (
    <>
      <header className="main-title">CV</header>
    </>
  );
}


export default CV;
```

```
1  function CV() {
2    return (
3      <>
4        <header className="main-title">CV</header>
5      </>
6    );
7  }
8
9  export default CV;
```

16.6 Add Route

```
import "./App.css";
import { BrowserRouter, Route, Routes } from
"react-router-dom";
import TopBar from "./layout/top-bar/top-bar";
import Sidenav from "./layout/sidenav/sidenav";
import { useState } from "react";
import Footer from "./layout/footer/footer";
```

```javascript
import Home from "./pages/home/home";
import About from "./pages/about/about";
import CV from "./pages/cv/cv";

function App() {
  const [opened, setOpened] = useState(false);

  return (
    <div>
      <BrowserRouter>
        <TopBar opened={opened}
setOpened={setOpened} />
        <Sidenav opened={opened}
setOpened={setOpened} />
        <main className="main">
          <Routes>
            <Route path="/" element={<Home />}
/>
            <Route path="/home" element={<Home
/>} />
            <Route path="/about"
element={<About />} />
            <Route path="/cv" element={<CV
/>} />
          </Routes>
        </main>
        <Footer />
      </BrowserRouter>
    </div>
  );
}

export default App;
```

```jsx
import "./App.css";
import { BrowserRouter, Route, Routes } from "react-router-dom";
import TopBar from "./layout/top-bar/top-bar";
import Sidenav from "./layout/sidenav/sidenav";
import { useState } from "react";
import Footer from "./layout/footer/footer";
import Home from "./pages/home/home";
import About from "./pages/about/about";
import CV from "./pages/cv/cv";

function App() {
  const [opened, setOpened] = useState(false);

  return (
    <div>
      <BrowserRouter>
        <TopBar opened={opened} setOpened={setOpened} />
        <Sidenav opened={opened} setOpened={setOpened} />
        <main className="main">
          <Routes>
            <Route path="/" element={<Home />} />
            <Route path="/home" element={<Home />} />
            <Route path="/about" element={<About />} />
            <Route path="/cv" element={<CV />} />
          </Routes>
        </main>
        <Footer />
      </BrowserRouter>
    </div>
  );
}

export default App;
```

Chapter 17: Experiences Data

17.1 Create It

In the "data" folder, create experiences.data.ts

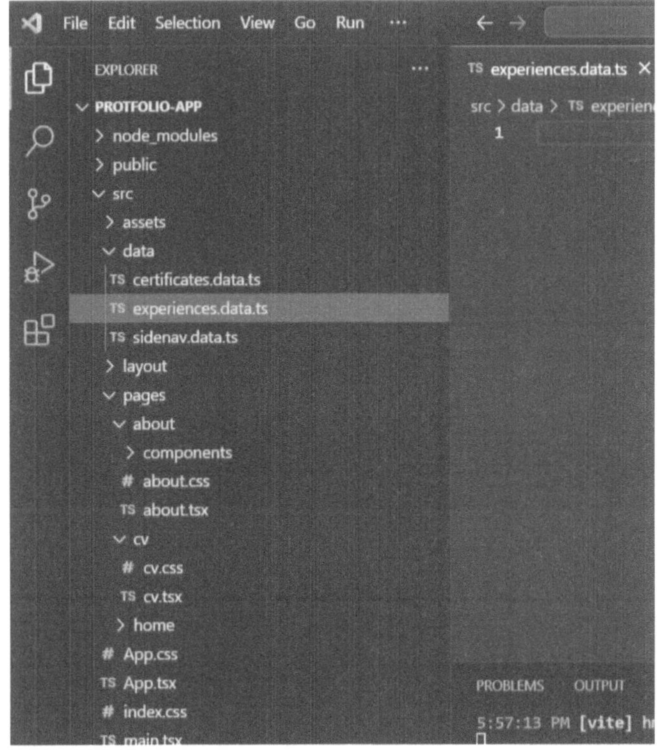

17.2 TS

```
export interface Experience {
```

```typescript
  title: string;
  subtitle: string;
  linesHeader: string;
  lines: string[];
}

export const EXPERIENCES: Experience[] = [
  {
    title: 'Senior Software Developer -
Angular',
    subtitle: '2019 - Present',
    linesHeader: 'Working for clients online',
    lines: [
      'Developing and implementing user
interface components',
      'Collaborating with cross-functional
teams to analyze requirements',
      'Designing and implementing scalable and
efficient solutions',
      'Writing clean, maintainable, and
testable code',
    ],
  },
  {
    title: 'Senior Software Developer -
Java/Angular',
    subtitle: '2017 - 2019',
    linesHeader: 'Work for the company
siParadigm',
    lines: [
      'Troubleshooting complex issues in
Angular applications',
      'Conducting code reviews to ensure code
quality and performance',
```

```javascript
      'Collaborating with UI/UX designers to
ensure the feasibility',
      'Optimizing application performance by
identifying bottlenecks',
    ],
  },
  {
    title: 'Senior Software Developer -
.NET/Angular',
    subtitle: '2014 - 2017',
    linesHeader: 'Work for clients online',
    lines: [
      'Integrating third-party libraries and
APIs into Angular applications',
      'Collaborating with backend developers to
design RESTful APIs',
      'Implementing and maintaining unit tests
and end-to-end tests',
      'Participating in Agile development
processes, including sprint planning',
    ],
  },
];
```

```typescript
export interface Experience {
  title: string;
  subtitle: string;
  linesHeader: string;
  lines: string[];
}

export const EXPERIENCES: Experience[] = [
  {
    title: 'Senior Software Developer - Angular',
    subtitle: '2019 - Present',
    linesHeader: 'Working for clients online',
    lines: [
      'Developing and implementing user interface components',
      'Collaborating with cross-functional teams to analyze requirements',
      'Designing and implementing scalable and efficient solutions',
      'Writing clean, maintainable, and testable code',
    ],
  },
  {
    title: 'Senior Software Developer - Java/Angular',
    subtitle: '2017 - 2019',
    linesHeader: 'Work for the company siParadigm',
    lines: [
      'Troubleshooting complex issues in Angular applications',
      'Conducting code reviews to ensure code quality and performance',
      'Collaborating with UI/UX designers to ensure the feasibility',
      'Optimizing application performance by identifying bottlenecks',
    ],
  },
  {
    title: 'Senior Software Developer - .NET/Angular',
    subtitle: '2014 - 2017',
    linesHeader: 'Work for clients online',
    lines: [
      'Integrating third-party libraries and APIs into Angular applications',
      'Collaborating with backend developers to design RESTful APIs',
      'Implementing and maintaining unit tests and end-to-end tests',
      'Participating in Agile development processes, including sprint planning',
    ],
  },
];
```

Chapter 18: [CV] Experiences Component

18.1 Preview

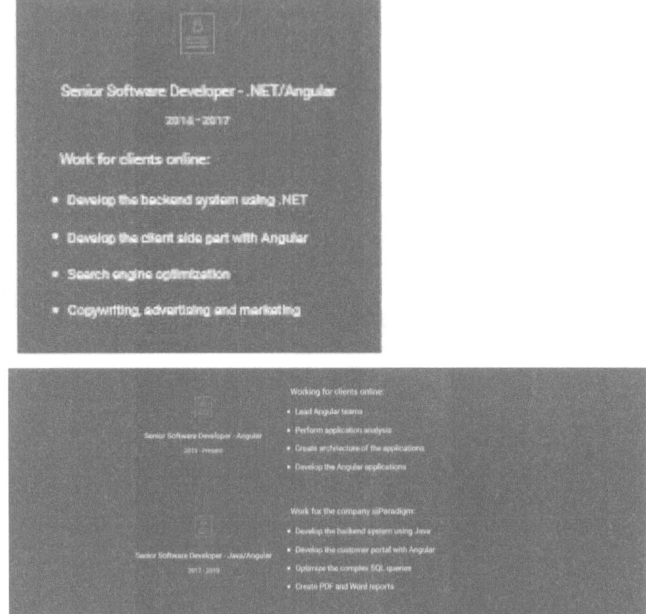

18.2 Create It

- Create a new "experiences" folder inside "pages/cv/components"

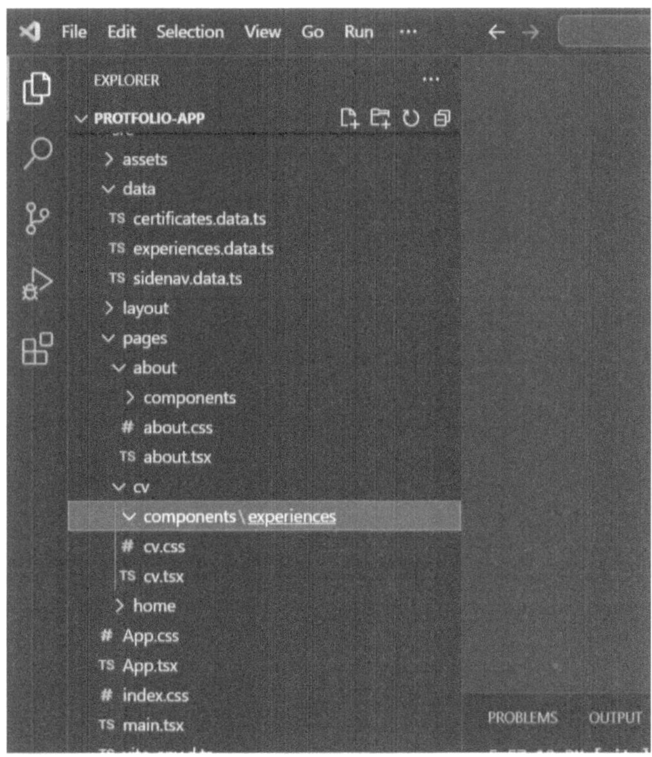

- Create experiences.tsx
- Create experiences.css

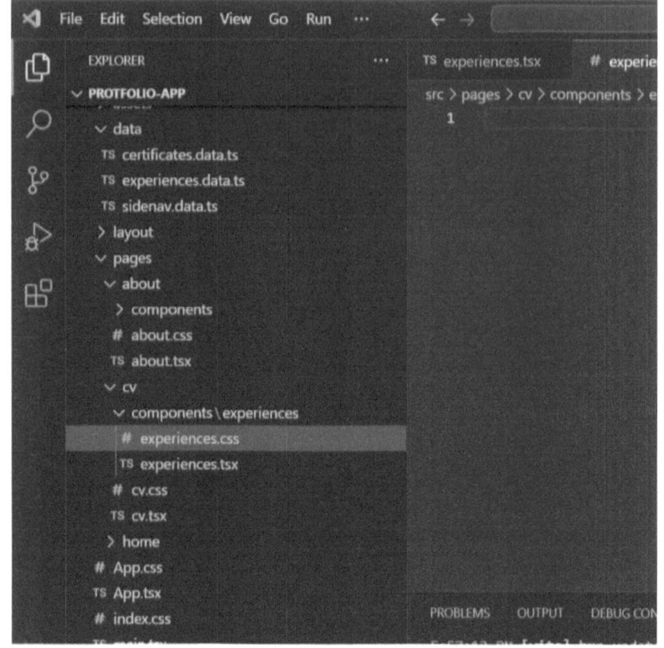

18.3 TSX

```tsx
import "./experiences.css";
import { EXPERIENCES, Experience } from
"../../../../data/experiences.data";

function Experiences() {
  const createExperienceLine = (line: string)
=> <span key={line}>{line}</span>;
  const createExperienceElement = (experience:
Experience) => (
    <section key={experience.title}
className="experience">
```

```jsx
      <div className="experience-header">
        <img className="experience-header-icon"
src="images/cv/cv.svg" />
        <div
className="experience-header-title">{experience
.title}</div>
        <div
className="experience-header-subtitle">{experie
nce.subtitle}</div>
      </div>
      <div className="experience-content">

<header>{experience.linesHeader}</header>

{experience.lines.map(createExperienceLine)}
      </div>
    </section>
  );

  return
<>{EXPERIENCES.map(createExperienceElement)}</>
;
}

export default Experiences;
```

```tsx
import "./experiences.css";
import { EXPERIENCES, Experience } from "../../../../data/experiences.data";

function Experiences() {
  const createExperienceLine = (line: string) => <span key={line}>{line}</span>;
  const createExperienceElement = (experience: Experience) => (
    <section key={experience.title} className="experience">
      <div className="experience-header">
        <img className="experience-header-icon" src="images/cv/cv.svg" />
        <div className="experience-header-title">{experience.title}</div>
        <div className="experience-header-subtitle">{experience.subtitle}</div>
      </div>
      <div className="experience-content">
        <header>{experience.linesHeader}</header>
        {experience.lines.map(createExperienceLine)}
      </div>
    </section>
  );

  return <>{EXPERIENCES.map(createExperienceElement)}</>;
}

export default Experiences;
```

18.4 CSS

```css
.experience {
  display: grid;
  padding: 10px 0px;
  margin-bottom: 40px;
  @media (min-width: 760px) {
    grid-template-columns: 40% 60%;
  }
}
.experience-header {
  display: flex;
  flex-direction: column;
  justify-content: center;
  align-items: center;
  gap: 10px;
  margin-top: -30px;
}
.experience-header-icon {
  width: 42px;
  opacity: 0.6;
```

```css
  margin-bottom: 20px;
}
.experience-header-title {
  font-size: 1.1em;
}
.experience-header-subtitle {
  font-size: 0.9em;
  opacity: 0.8;
}
.experience-content {
  display: flex;
  flex-direction: column;
  justify-content: flex-start;
  align-items: flex-start;
  width: 100%;
  margin-top: 20px;
  @media (min-width: 760px) {
    margin-top: 0px;
  }
}
.experience-content header {
  text-align: left;
  font-size: 1.1em;
  margin-bottom: 20px;
  padding-left: 10px;
  @media (min-width: 760px) {
    font-size: 1.2em;
  }
}
.experience-content span {
  font-size: 16px;
  margin: 8px 0px;
  margin-top: -6px;
  width: 100%;
```

```css
    text-align: left;
    line-height: 40px;
    @media (min-width: 760px) {
      font-size: 18px;
    }
}
.experience-content span::before {
    content: "•";
    margin-right: 10px;
    font-size: 1.8em;
    vertical-align: bottom;
}
```

```css
.experience {
  display: grid;
  padding: 10px 0px;
  margin-bottom: 40px;
  @media (min-width: 760px) {
    grid-template-columns: 40% 60%;
  }
}
.experience-header {
  display: flex;
  flex-direction: column;
  justify-content: center;
  align-items: center;
  gap: 10px;
  margin-top: -30px;
}
.experience-header-icon {
  width: 42px;
  opacity: 0.6;
  margin-bottom: 20px;
}
.experience-header-title {
  font-size: 1.1em;
}
.experience-header-subtitle {
  font-size: 0.9em;
  opacity: 0.8;
}
.experience-content {
  display: flex;
  flex-direction: column;
  justify-content: flex-start;
  align-items: flex-start;
  width: 100%;
  margin-top: 20px;
  @media (min-width: 760px) {
    margin-top: 0px;
  }
}
.experience-content header {
  text-align: left;
  font-size: 1.1em;
  margin-bottom: 20px;
  padding-left: 10px;
  @media (min-width: 760px) {
    font-size: 1.2em;
  }
}
.experience-content span {
  font-size: 16px;
  margin: 8px 0px;
  margin-top: -6px;
  width: 100%;
  text-align: left;
  line-height: 40px;
  @media (min-width: 760px) {
    font-size: 18px;
  }
}
.experience-content span::before {
  content: "•";
  margin-right: 10px;
  font-size: 1.8em;
  vertical-align: bottom;
}
```

18.5 Use It

```
import Experiences from
"./components/experiences/experiences";
```

```
function CV() {
  return (
    <>
      <header
className="main-title">CV</header>
      <Experiences />
    </>
  );
}


export default CV;
```

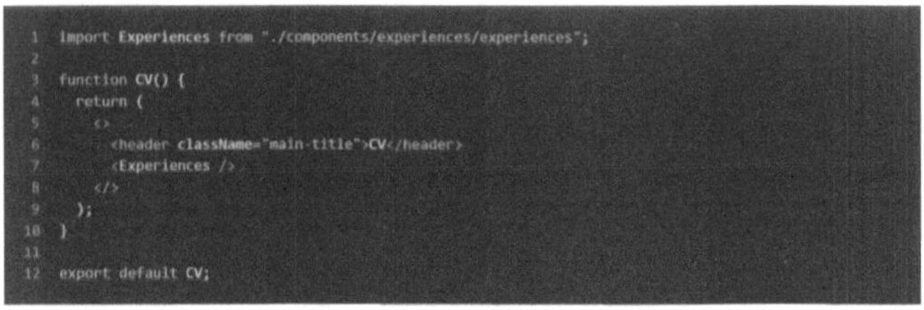

```
1   import Experiences from "./components/experiences/experiences";
2
3   function CV() {
4     return (
5       <>
6         <header className="main-title">CV</header>
7         <Experiences />
8       </>
9     );
10  }
11
12  export default CV;
```

Chapter 19: [CV] Download CV Component

19.1 Preview

19.2 Create It

- Create folder "download-cv" inside "pages/cv/components"

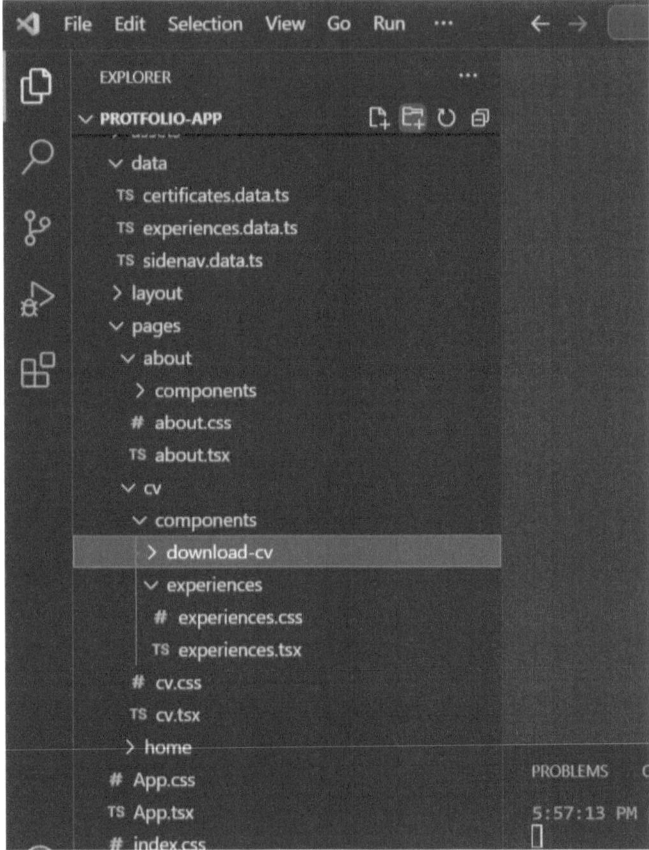

- Create download-cv.tsx
- Create download-cv.css

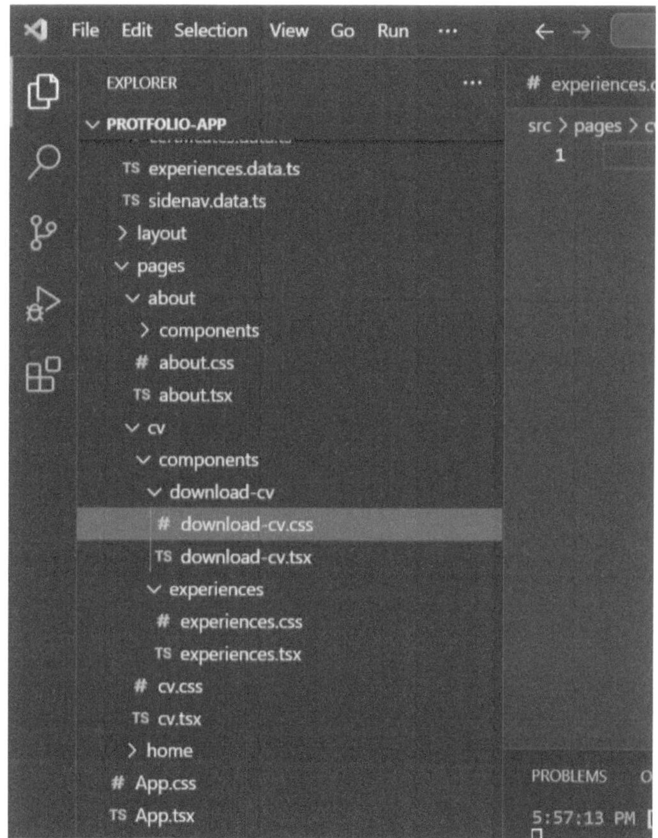

19.3 TSX

```tsx
import "./download-cv.css";

function DownloadCV() {
  return (
    <section className="download-cv">
```

```jsx
        <a href="files/cv/Abdelfattah-CV.pdf"
download>
          <img
src="images/cv/Abdelfattah-CV-1.jpg"
className="cv-imagg" />
        </a>
        <a href="files/cv/Abdelfattah-CV.pdf"
download>
          <img
src="images/cv/Abdelfattah-CV-2.jpg"
className="cv-imagg" />
        </a>
        <a href="files/Abdelfattah-CV.pdf"
className="download-button" download>
          Download
        </a>
      </section>
  );
}


export default DownloadCV;
```

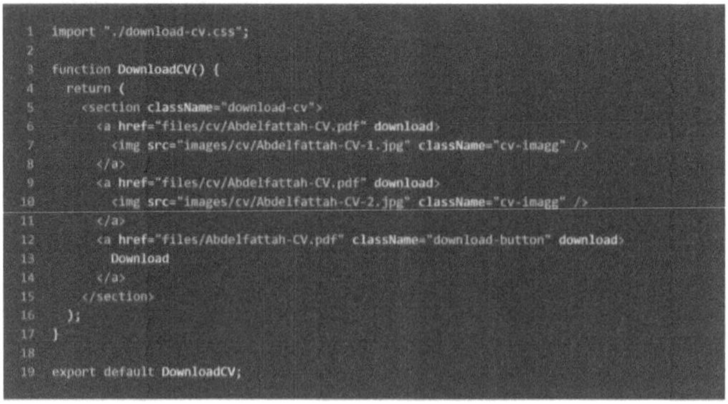

```jsx
1   import "./download-cv.css";
2
3   function DownloadCV() {
4     return (
5       <section className="download-cv">
6         <a href="files/cv/Abdelfattah-CV.pdf" download>
7           <img src="images/cv/Abdelfattah-CV-1.jpg" className="cv-imagg" />
8         </a>
9         <a href="files/cv/Abdelfattah-CV.pdf" download>
10          <img src="images/cv/Abdelfattah-CV-2.jpg" className="cv-imagg" />
11        </a>
12        <a href="files/Abdelfattah-CV.pdf" className="download-button" download>
13          Download
14        </a>
15      </section>
16    );
17  }
18
19  export default DownloadCV;
```

19.4 CSS

```css
.download-cv {
  display: flex;
  margin-top: 100px;
  column-gap: 30px;
  row-gap: 10px;
  flex-direction: column;
  justify-content: center;
  align-items: center;
  @media (min-width: 760px) {
    flex-direction: row;
  }
}
.cv-imagg {
  width: 160px;
}
.download-button {
  background-color: var(--accent-color-1);
  color: var(--accent-color-2) !important;
  border-radius: 8px;
  padding: 6px 20px;
  font-size: 0.9em;
  margin-top: 6px;
}
```

```css
1   .download-cv {
2     display: flex;
3     margin-top: 100px;
4     column-gap: 30px;
5     row-gap: 10px;
6     flex-direction: column;
7     justify-content: center;
8     align-items: center;
9     @media (min-width: 760px) {
10      flex-direction: row;
11    }
12  }
13  .cv-imagg {
14    width: 160px;
15  }
16  .download-button {
17    background-color: var(--accent-color-1);
18    color: var(--accent-color-2) !important;
19    border-radius: 8px;
20    padding: 6px 20px;
21    font-size: 0.9em;
22    margin-top: 6px;
23  }
```

19.5 Use It

```jsx
import DownloadCV from
"./components/download-cv/download-cv";
import Experiences from
"./components/experiences/experiences";

function CV() {
  return (
    <>
      <header
className="main-title">CV</header>
      <Experiences />
      <DownloadCV />
    </>
  );
}

export default CV;
```

```jsx
import DownloadCV from "./components/download-cv/download-cv";
import Experiences from "./components/experiences/experiences";

function CV() {
  return (
    <>
      <header className="main-title">CV</header>
      <Experiences />
      <DownloadCV />
    </>
  );
}

export default CV;
```

Chapter 20: Projects Page

20.1 Preview

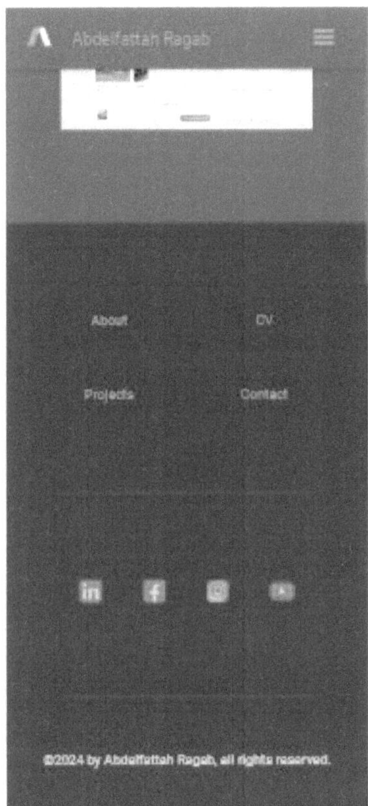

Abdelfattah Ragab
About
CV
Projects
Contact

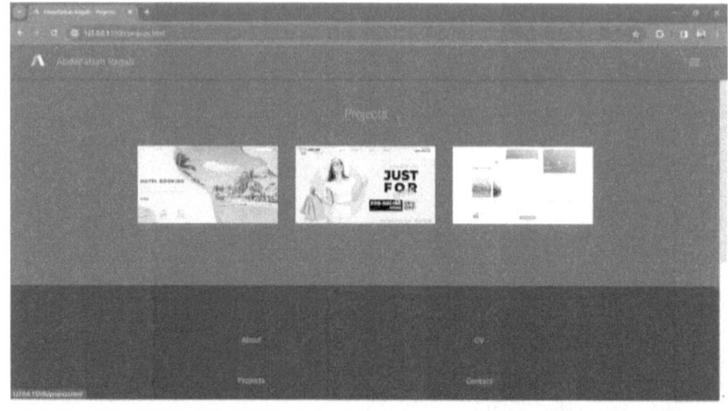

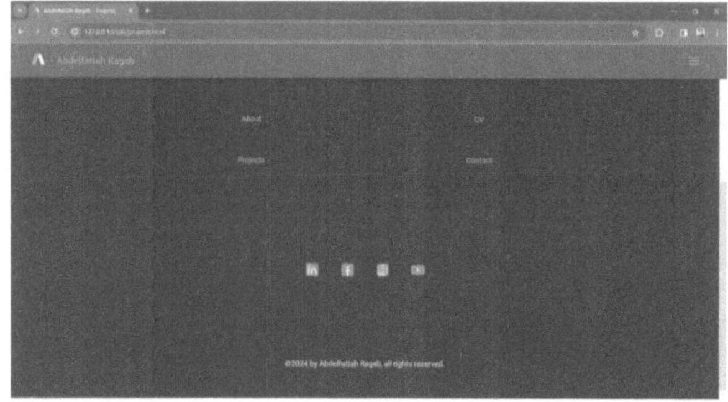

20.2 Page Outline

```
<ProjectGallery />
```

20.3 Create It

- Create a new folder "projects" inside "pages"

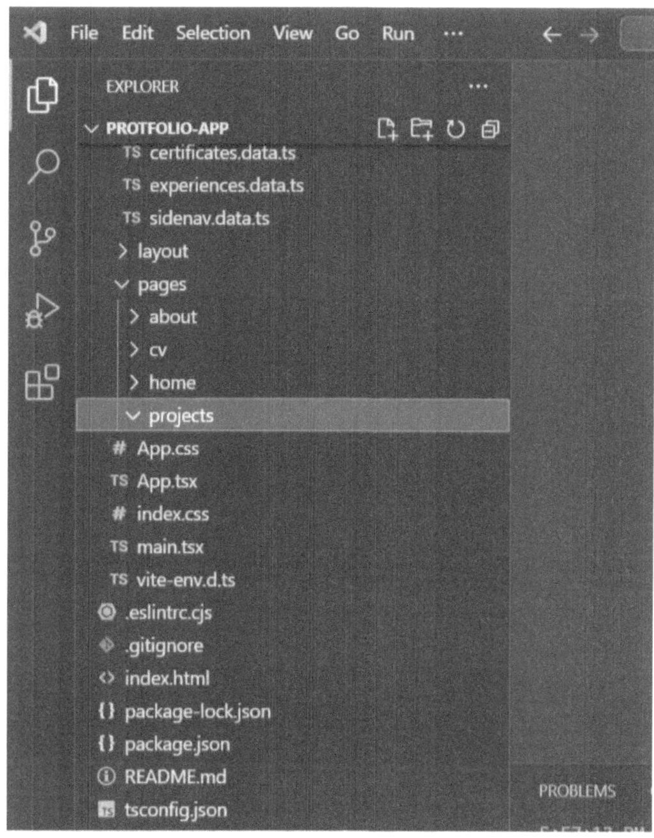

- Create projects.tsx
- Create projects.css

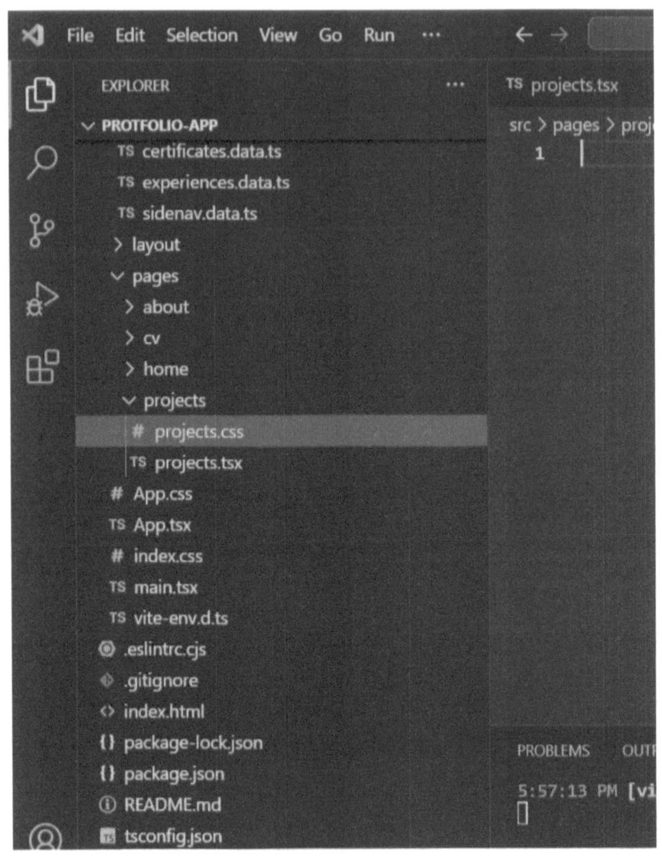

20.4 TSX

```
function Projects() {
  return <></>;
}

export default Projects;
```

```
1  function Projects() {
2    return <></>;
3  }
4
5  export default Projects;
```

20.5 Set Title

```
function Projects() {
  return (
    <>
      <header
className="main-title">Projects</header>
    </>
  );
}

export default Projects;
```

```
1  function Projects() {
2    return (
3      <>
4        <header className="main-title">Projects</header>
5      </>
6    );
7  }
8
9  export default Projects;
```

20.6 Add Route

```
import "./App.css";
import { BrowserRouter, Route, Routes } from
"react-router-dom";
import TopBar from "./layout/top-bar/top-bar";
import Sidenav from "./layout/sidenav/sidenav";
import { useState } from "react";
```

```jsx
import Footer from "./layout/footer/footer";
import Home from "./pages/home/home";
import About from "./pages/about/about";
import CV from "./pages/cv/cv";
import Projects from
"./pages/projects/projects";

function App() {
  const [opened, setOpened] = useState(false);

  return (
    <div>
      <BrowserRouter>
        <TopBar opened={opened}
setOpened={setOpened} />
        <Sidenav opened={opened}
setOpened={setOpened} />
        <main className="main">
          <Routes>
            <Route path="/" element={<Home />}
/>
            <Route path="/home" element={<Home
/>} />
            <Route path="/about"
element={<About />} />
            <Route path="/cv" element={<CV />}
/>
            <Route path="/projects"
element={<Projects />} />
          </Routes>
        </main>
        <Footer />
      </BrowserRouter>
    </div>
```

```
  );
}


export default App;
```

```jsx
1   import "./App.css";
2   import { BrowserRouter, Route, Routes } from "react-router-dom";
3   import TopBar from "./layout/top-bar/top-bar";
4   import Sidenav from "./layout/sidenav/sidenav";
5   import { useState } from "react";
6   import Footer from "./layout/footer/footer";
7   import Home from "./pages/home/home";
8   import About from "./pages/about/about";
9   import CV from "./pages/cv/cv";
10  import Projects from "./pages/projects/projects";
11
12  function App() {
13    const [opened, setOpened] = useState(false);
14
15    return (
16      <div>
17        <BrowserRouter>
18          <TopBar opened={opened} setOpened={setOpened} />
19          <Sidenav opened={opened} setOpened={setOpened} />
20          <main className="main">
21            <Routes>
22              <Route path="/" element={<Home />} />
23              <Route path="/home" element={<Home />} />
24              <Route path="/about" element={<About />} />
25              <Route path="/cv" element={<CV />} />
26              <Route path="/projects" element={<Projects />} />
27            </Routes>
28          </main>
29          <Footer />
30        </BrowserRouter>
31      </div>
32    );
33  }
34
35  export default App;
```

Chapter 21: Project Gallery Data

21.1 Create It

Create the file project-gallery.data.ts in "data"

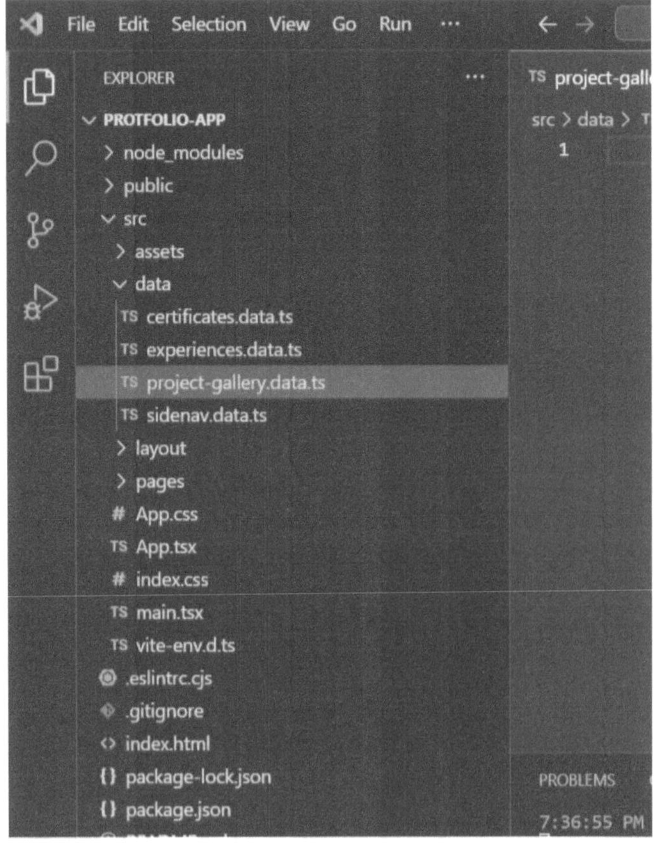

21.2 TS

```typescript
export interface Project {
  title: string;
  imageUrl: string;
}

export const PROJECTS: Project[] = [
  { title: 'Project 1', imageUrl:
'assets/images/projects/project-1.jpg' },
  { title: 'Project 2', imageUrl:
'assets/images/projects/project-2.jpg' },
  { title: 'Project 3', imageUrl:
'assets/images/projects/project-3.jpg' },
];
```

Chapter 22: [Projects] Project Gallery Component

22.1 Preview

22.2 Create It

- Create a new folder "project-gallery" in "pages/projects/components"

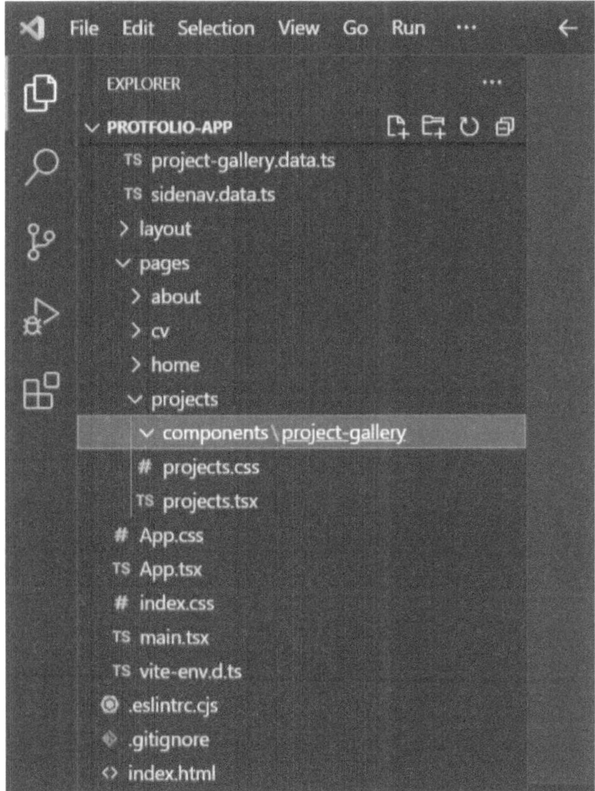

- Create project-gallery.tsx
- Create project-gallery.css

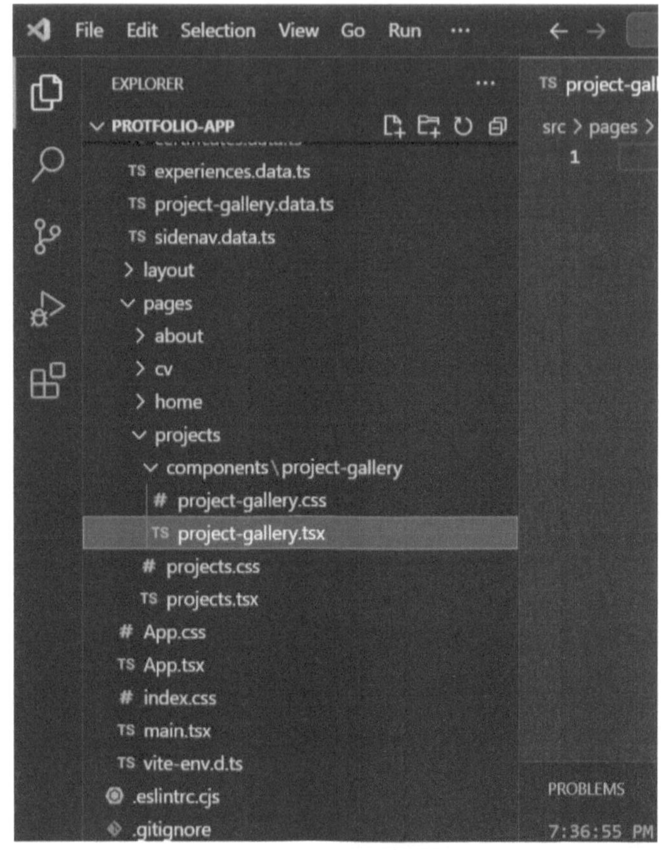

22.3 TSX

```tsx
import { PROJECTS, Project } from
"../../../../data/project-gallery.data";
import "./project-gallery.css";

function ProjectGallery() {
```

```jsx
  const createProjectElement = (project:
Project) => (
    <img
      key={project.title}
      src={project.imageUrl}
      alt={project.title}
      title={project.title}
      className="project link"
    />
  );
  return <div
className="projects">{PROJECTS.map(createProjec
tElement)}</div>;
}

export default ProjectGallery;
```

```jsx
1   import { PROJECTS, Project } from "../../../../data/project-gallery.data";
2   import "./project-gallery.css";
3
4   function ProjectGallery() {
5     const createProjectElement = (project: Project) => (
6       <img
7         key={project.title}
8         src={project.imageUrl}
9         alt={project.title}
10        title={project.title}
11        className="project link"
12      />
13    );
14    return <div className="projects">{PROJECTS.map(createProjectElement)}</div>;
15  }
16
17  export default ProjectGallery;
```

22.4 CSS

```css
.projects {
  display: grid;
  gap: 40px;
  place-items: center center;
  @media (min-width: 760px) {
    grid-template-columns: repeat(3, 1fr);
```

```css
    gap: 30px;
  }
}
.project {
  width: 300px;
}
```

```css
1   .projects {
2     display: grid;
3     gap: 40px;
4     place-items: center center;
5     @media (min-width: 760px) {
6       grid-template-columns: repeat(3, 1fr);
7       gap: 30px;
8     }
9   }
10  .project {
11    width: 300px;
12  }
```

22.5 Use It

```jsx
import ProjectGallery from
"./components/project-gallery/project-gallery";

function Projects() {
  return (
    <>
      <header
className="main-title">Projects</header>
      <ProjectGallery />
    </>
  );
}

export default Projects;
```

```jsx
import ProjectGallery from "./components/project-gallery/project-gallery";

function Projects() {
  return (
    <>
      <header className="main-title">Projects</header>
      <ProjectGallery />
    </>
  );
}

export default Projects;
```

Chapter 23: Contact Page

23.1 Preview

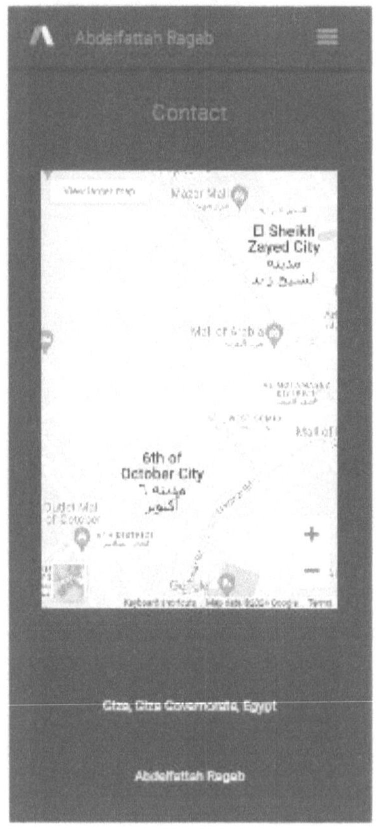

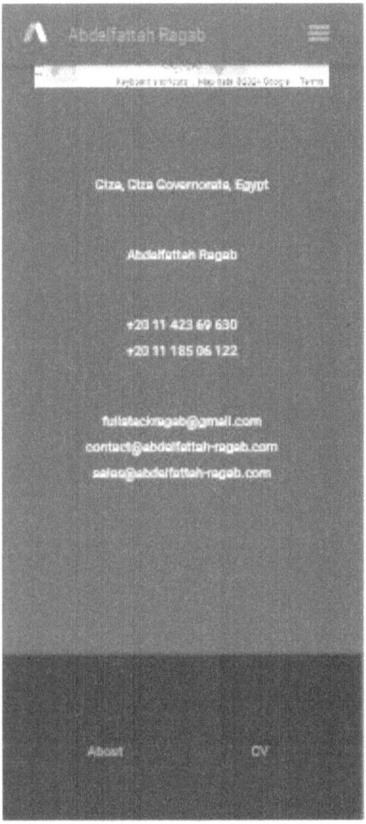
Abdelfattah Ragab
Giza, Giza Governorate, Egypt
Abdelfattah Ragab
+20 11 423 69 630
+20 11 185 06 122
fullstackragab@gmail.com
contact@abdelfattah-ragab.com
sales@abdelfattah-ragab.com
About
CV

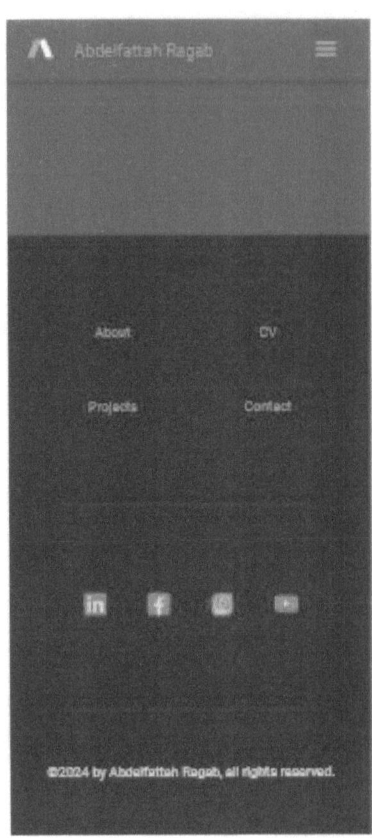
Abdelfattah Ragab
About
CV
Projects
Contact
©2024 by Abdelfattah Ragab, all rights reserved.

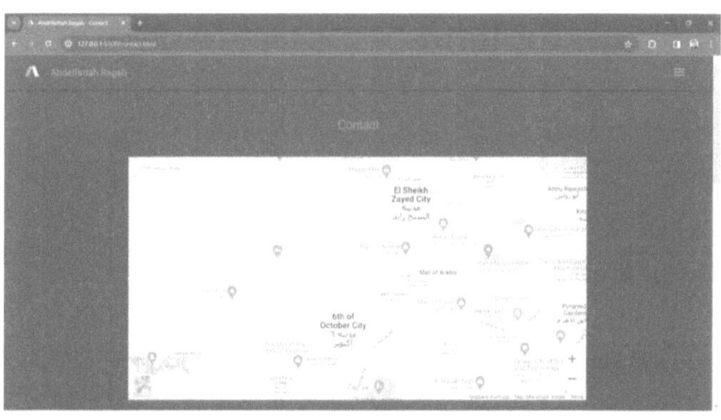

Abdelfattah Ragab
Contact
El Sheikh
Zayed City
6th of
October City
Mall of Arabia

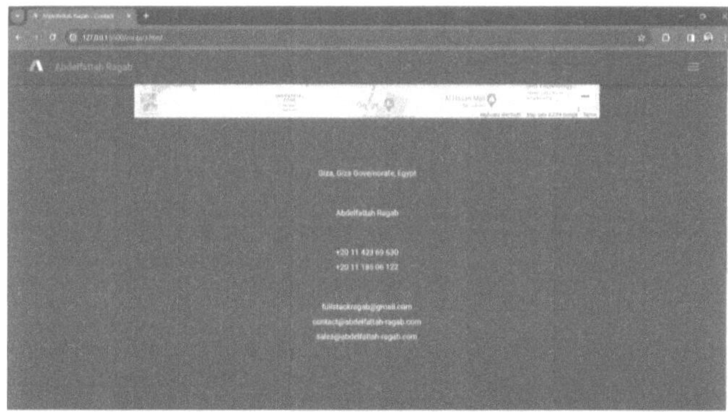

Abdelfattah Ragab
Giza, Giza Governorate, Egypt
Abdelfattah Ragab
+20 11 423 69 530
+20 11 186 06 122
fullstackragab@gmail.com
contact@abdelfattah-ragab.com
sales@abdelfattah-ragab.com

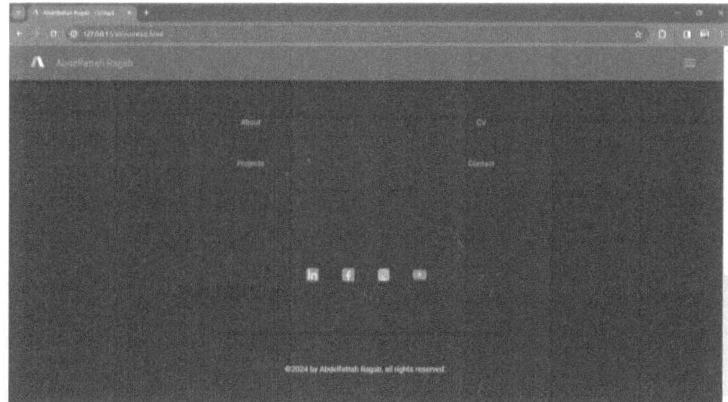

Abdelfattah Ragab
About   CV
Projects   Contact
©2024 by Abdelfattah Ragab, all rights reserved.

23.2 Page Outline

```
<LocationMap />
<ContactInfo />
```

23.3 Create It

- Create new folder "contact" in "pages"

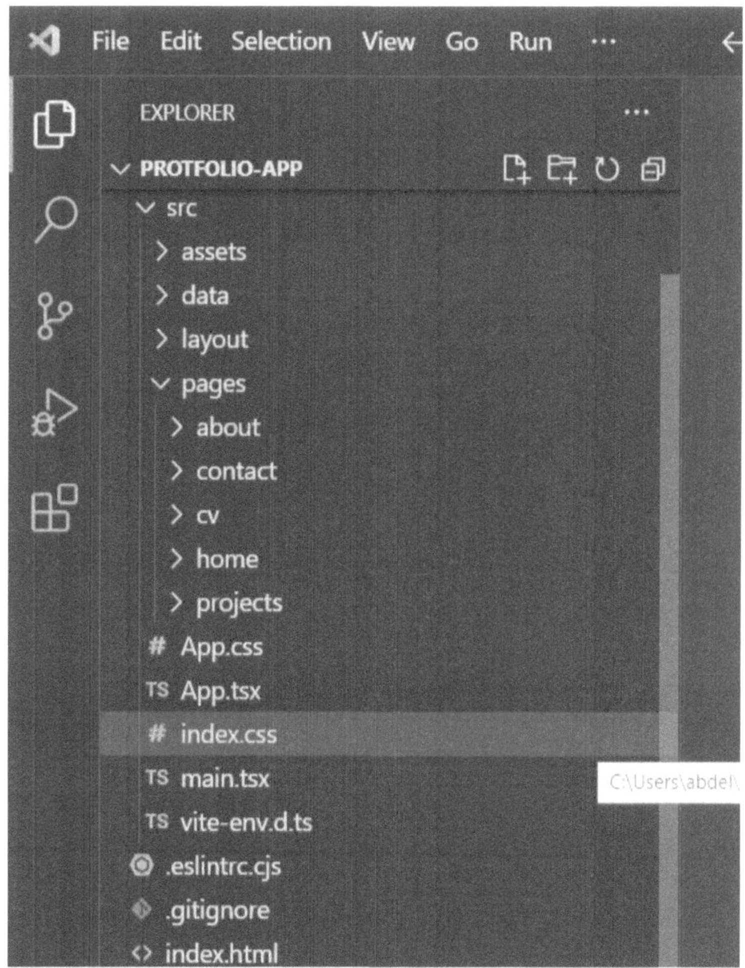

- Create contact.tsx
- Create contact.css

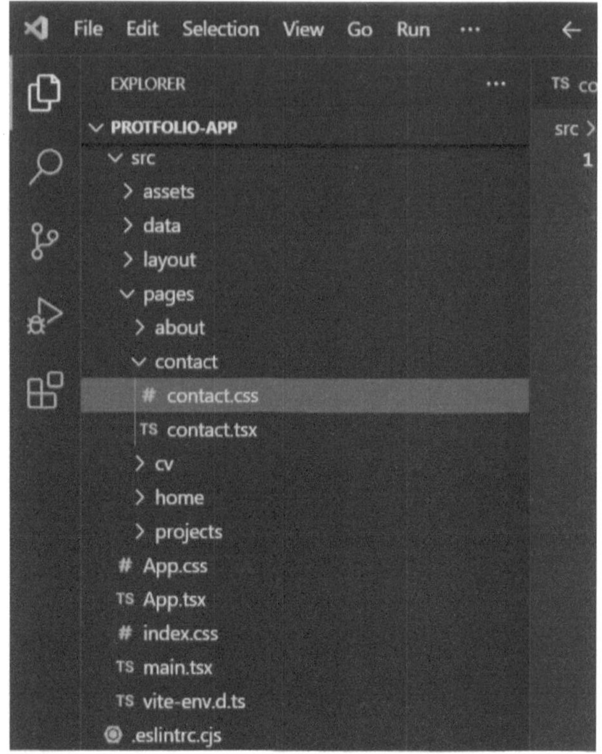

23.4 TSX

```
function Contact() {
  return <></>;
}

export default Contact;
```

```
1   function Contact() {
2     return <></>;
3   }
4
5   export default Contact;
```

23.5 CSS

Nothing

23.6 Set Title

```
function Contact() {
  return (
    <>
      <header
className="main-title">Contact</header>
    </>
  );
}

export default Contact;
```

```
1   function Contact() {
2     return (
3       <>
4         <header className="main-title">Contact</header>
5       </>
6     );
7   }
8
9   export default Contact;
```

23.7 Add Route

```
import "./App.css";
```

```jsx
import { BrowserRouter, Routes, Route } from
"react-router-dom";
import Footer from "./layout/footer/footer";
import "./layout/top-bar/top-bar";
import TopBar from "./layout/top-bar/top-bar";
import About from "./pages/about/about";
import Contact from "./pages/contact/contact";
import CV from "./pages/cv/cv";
import Home from "./pages/home/home";
import Projects from
"./pages/projects/projects";
import Sidenav from "./layout/sidenav/sidenav";
import { useState } from "react";

function App() {
  const [opened, setOpened] = useState(false);
  return (
    <div>
      <BrowserRouter>
        <TopBar opened={opened}
setOpened={setOpened} />
        <Sidenav opened={opened}
setOpened={setOpened} />
        <main className="main">
          <Routes>
            <Route path="/" element={<Home />}
/>
            <Route path="/home" element={<Home
/>} />
            <Route path="/about"
element={<About />} />
            <Route path="/cv" element={<CV />}
/>
```

```jsx
            <Route path="/projects" element={<Projects />} />
            <Route path="/contact" element={<Contact />} />
          </Routes>
        </main>
        <Footer />
      </BrowserRouter>
    </div>
  );
}

export default App;
```

```jsx
1   import "./App.css";
2   import { BrowserRouter, Routes, Route } from "react-router-dom";
3   import Footer from "./layout/footer/footer";
4   import "./layout/top-bar/top-bar";
5   import TopBar from "./layout/top-bar/top-bar";
6   import About from "./pages/about/about";
7   import Contact from "./pages/contact/contact";
8   import CV from "./pages/cv/cv";
9   import Home from "./pages/home/home";
10  import Projects from "./pages/projects/projects";
11  import Sidenav from "./layout/sidenav/sidenav";
12  import { useState } from "react";
13
14  function App() {
15    const [opened, setOpened] = useState(false);
16    return (
17      <div>
18        <BrowserRouter>
19          <TopBar opened={opened} setOpened={setOpened} />
20          <Sidenav opened={opened} setOpened={setOpened} />
21          <main className="main">
22            <Routes>
23              <Route path="/" element={<Home />} />
24              <Route path="/home" element={<Home />} />
25              <Route path="/about" element={<About />} />
26              <Route path="/cv" element={<CV />} />
27              <Route path="/projects" element={<Projects />} />
28              <Route path="/contact" element={<Contact />} />
29            </Routes>
30          </main>
31          <Footer />
32        </BrowserRouter>
33      </div>
34    );
35  }
36
37  export default App;
38
```

Chapter 24: [Contact] Location Map Component

24.1 Preview

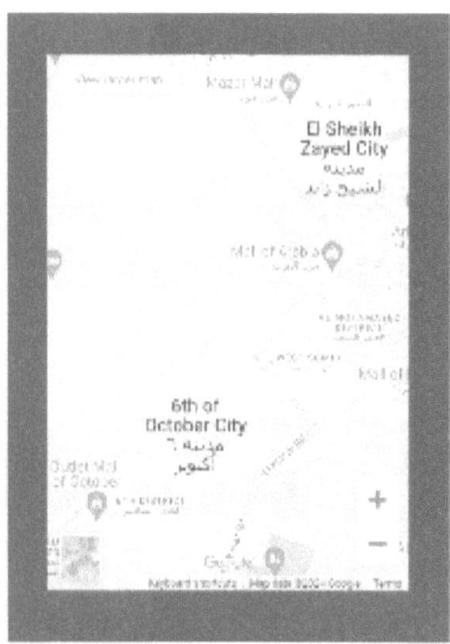

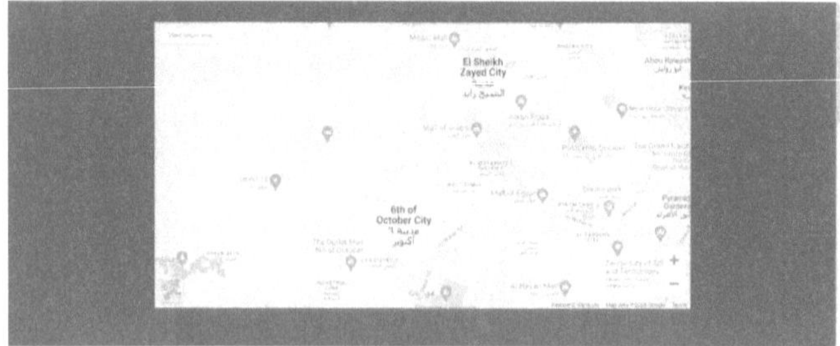

24.2 Create It

- Create folder "location-map" inside "pages/contact/components"

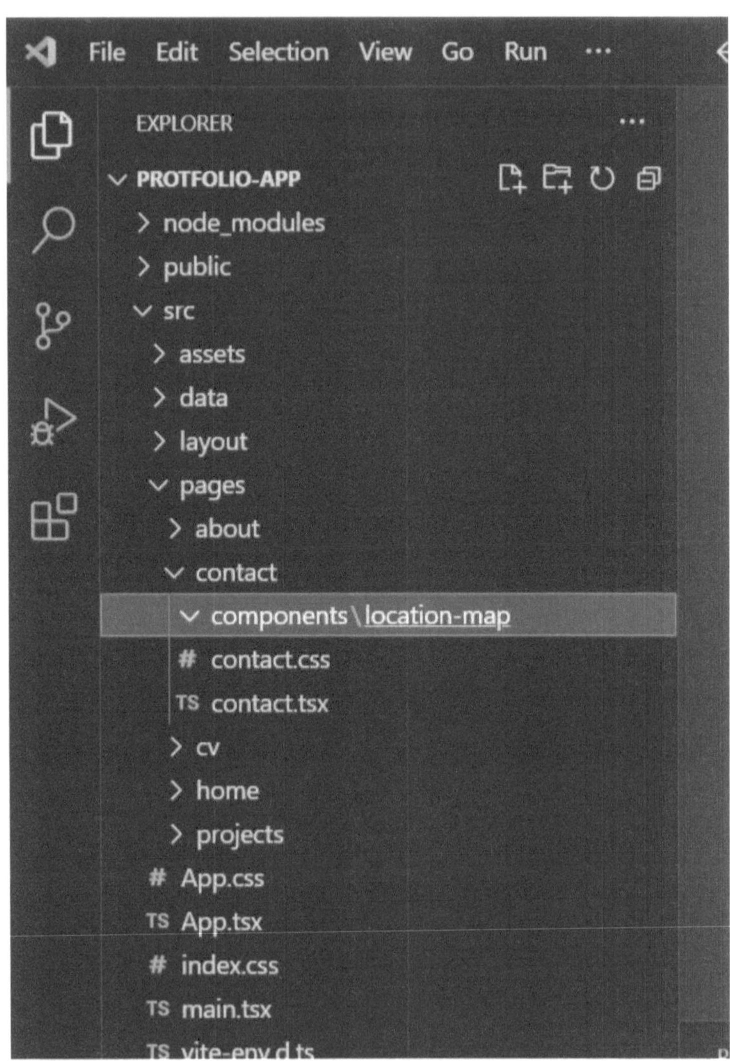

- Create location-map.tsx
- Create location-map.css

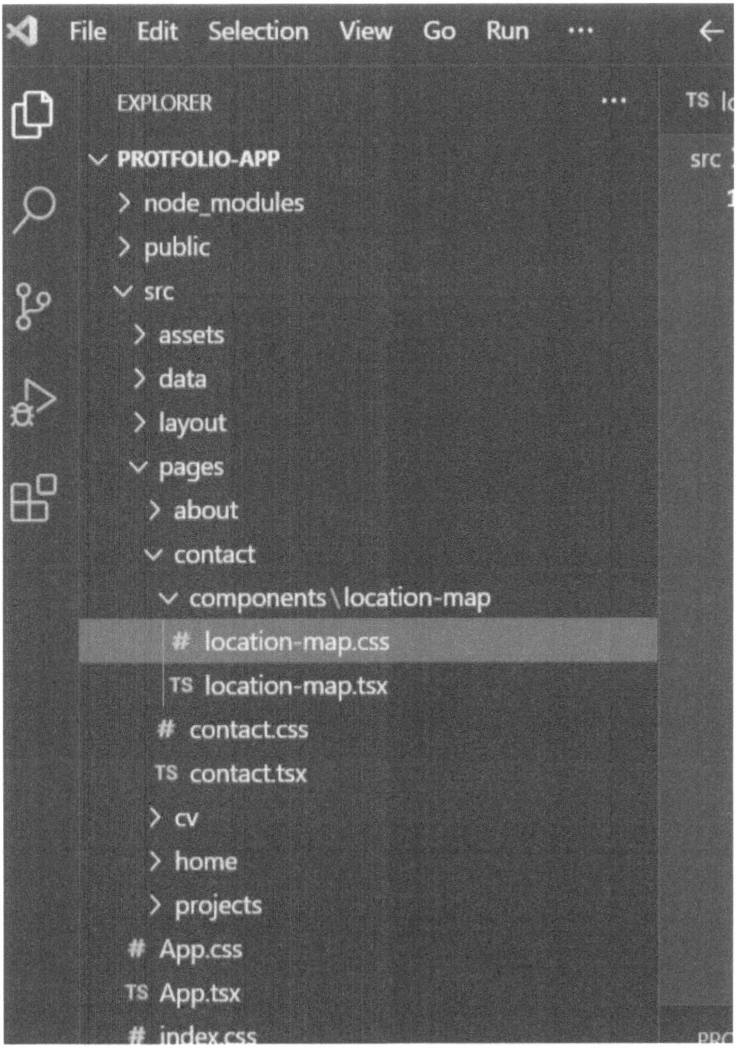

File   Edit   Selection   View   Go   Run   ···   ←

EXPLORER   ···   TS lo

PROTFOLIO-APP   src
  > node_modules   1
  > public
  ∨ src
    > assets
    > data
    > layout
    ∨ pages
      > about
      ∨ contact
        ∨ components\location-map
            # location-map.css
            TS location-map.tsx
          # contact.css
          TS contact.tsx
        > cv
        > home
        > projects
      # App.css
      TS App.tsx
      # index.css

24.3 TSX

```tsx
import "./location-map.css";

function LocationMap() {
  return (
    <iframe

src="https://www.google.com/maps/embed?pb=!1m14!1m12!1m3!1d86507.44890895384!2d30.940485229641485!3d29.992115477340583!2m3!1f0!2f0!3f0!3m2!1i1024!2i768!4f13.1!5e0!3m2!1sen!2seg!4v16795964244897!5m2!1sen!2seg"
      className="map"
      allowFullScreen={true}
      loading="lazy"

referrerPolicy="no-referrer-when-downgrade"
    ></iframe>
  );
}

export default LocationMap;
```


```tsx
1   import "./location-map.css";
2
3   function LocationMap() {
4     return (
5       <iframe
6         src="https://www.google.com/maps/embed?pb=!1m14!1m12!1m3!1d86507.44890895384!2d30.9404
8522964148513d29.99211547734058312m3!1f0!2f0!3f0!3m2!1i1024!2i768!4f13.1!5e0!3m2!1sen!2seg!4
v1679596424897!5m2!1sen!2seg"
7         className="map"
8         allowFullScreen={true}
9         loading="lazy"
10        referrerPolicy="no-referrer-when-downgrade"
11      ></iframe>
12    );
13  }
14
15  export default LocationMap;
```

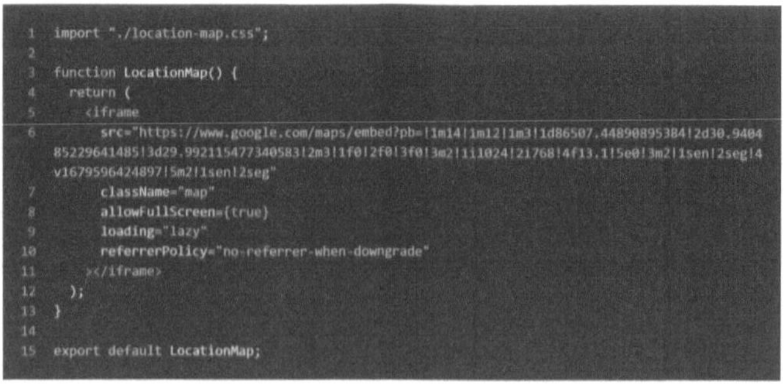

24.4 CSS

```css
.map {
  border: 0;
  background-image:
url(/assets/images/other/loading.gif);
  background-repeat: no-repeat;
  background-size: 50px 50px;
  background-position: center top;
  width: 100%;
  height: 500px;
}
```

```css
1   .map {
2     border: 0;
3     background-image: url(/assets/images/other/loading.gif);
4     background-repeat: no-repeat;
5     background-size: 50px 50px;
6     background-position: center top;
7     width: 100%;
8     height: 500px;
9   }
```

24.5 Use It

```jsx
import LocationMap from
"./components/location-map/location-map";

function Contact() {
  return (
    <>
      <header
className="main-title">Contact</header>
      <LocationMap />
    </>
  );
}
```

```
export default Contact;
```

```jsx
 1  import LocationMap from "./components/location-map/location-map";
 2
 3  function Contact() {
 4    return (
 5      <>
 6        <header className="main-title">Contact</header>
 7        <LocationMap />
 8      </>
 9    );
10  }
11
12  export default Contact;
```

Chapter 25: [Contact] Contact Info Component

25.1 Preview

25.2 Create It

- Create folder "contact-info" inside "pages/contact/components"

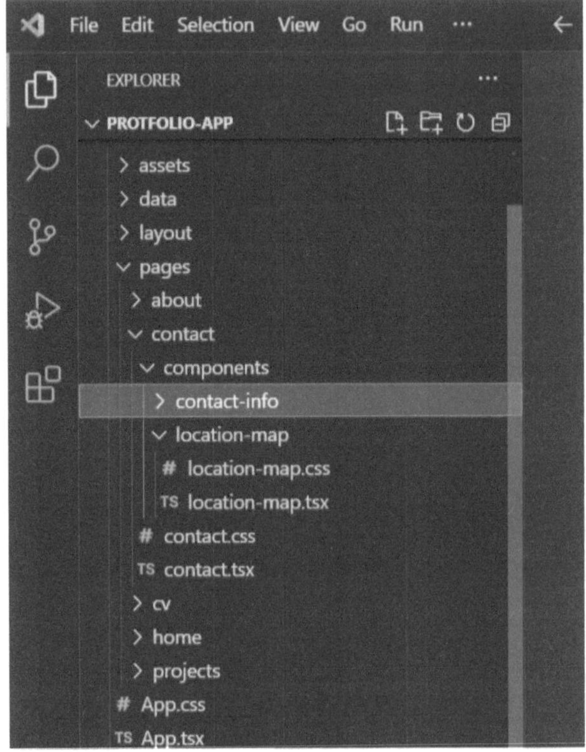

- Create contact-info.tsx
- Create contact-info.css

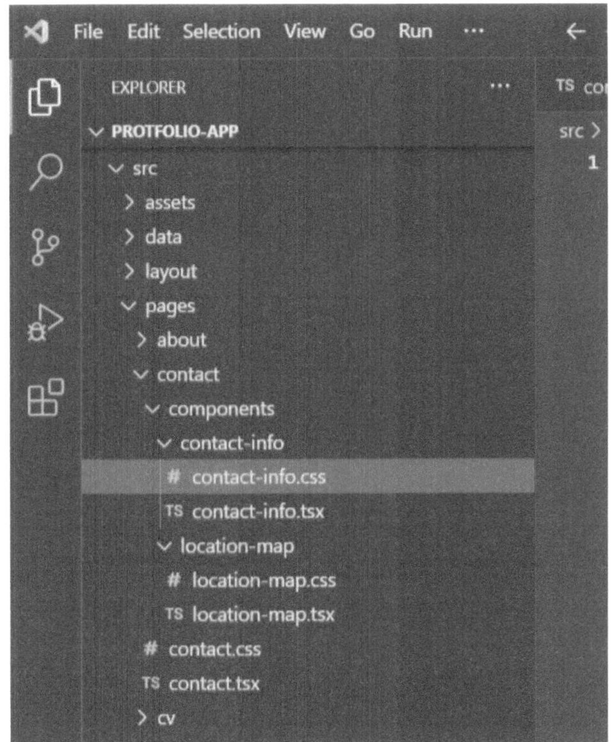

25.3 TSX

```tsx
import "./contact-info.css";

function ContactInfo() {
  return (
    <section className="contact-info">
      <p>Giza, Giza Governorate, Egypt</p>
      <p>Abdelfattah Ragab</p>
      <p>
        +20 11 423 69 630
```

```jsx
        <br />
        +20 11 185 06 122
      </p>
      <p>
        fullstackragab&#64;gmail.com
        <br />
        contact&#64;abdelfattah-ragab.com
        <br />
        sales&#64;abdelfattah-ragab.com
      </p>
    </section>
  );
}

export default ContactInfo;
```

```jsx
1   import "./contact-info.css";
2
3   function ContactInfo() {
4     return (
5       <section className="contact-info">
6         <p>Giza, Giza Governorate, Egypt</p>
7         <p>Abdelfattah Ragab</p>
8         <p>
9           +20 11 423 69 630
10          <br />
11          +20 11 185 06 122
12        </p>
13        <p>
14          fullstackragab&#64;gmail.com
15          <br />
16          contact&#64;abdelfattah-ragab.com
17          <br />
18          sales&#64;abdelfattah-ragab.com
19        </p>
20      </section>
21    );
22  }
23
24  export default ContactInfo;
```

25.4 CSS

```css
.contact-info {
```

```css
  padding: 40px 0px;
}
.contact-info p {
  margin: 50px 0px;
  line-height: 30px;
  text-align: center;
}
```

```
1   .contact-info {
2     padding: 40px 0px;
3   }
4   .contact-info p {
5     margin: 50px 0px;
6     line-height: 30px;
7     text-align: center;
8   }
```

25.5 Use It

```jsx
import ContactInfo from
"./components/contact-info/contact-info";
import LocationMap from
"./components/location-map/location-map";

function Contact() {
  return (
    <>
      <header
className="main-title">Contact</header>
      <LocationMap />
      <ContactInfo />
    </>
  );
}


export default Contact;
```

```jsx
import ContactInfo from "./components/contact-info/contact-info";
import LocationMap from "./components/location-map/location-map";

function Contact() {
  return (
    <>
      <header className="main-title">Contact</header>
      <LocationMap />
      <ContactInfo />
    </>
  );
}

export default Contact;
```

Chapter 26: ScrollToTop

26.1 Create It

- Create a new file scroll-to-top.tsx at root folder "src"

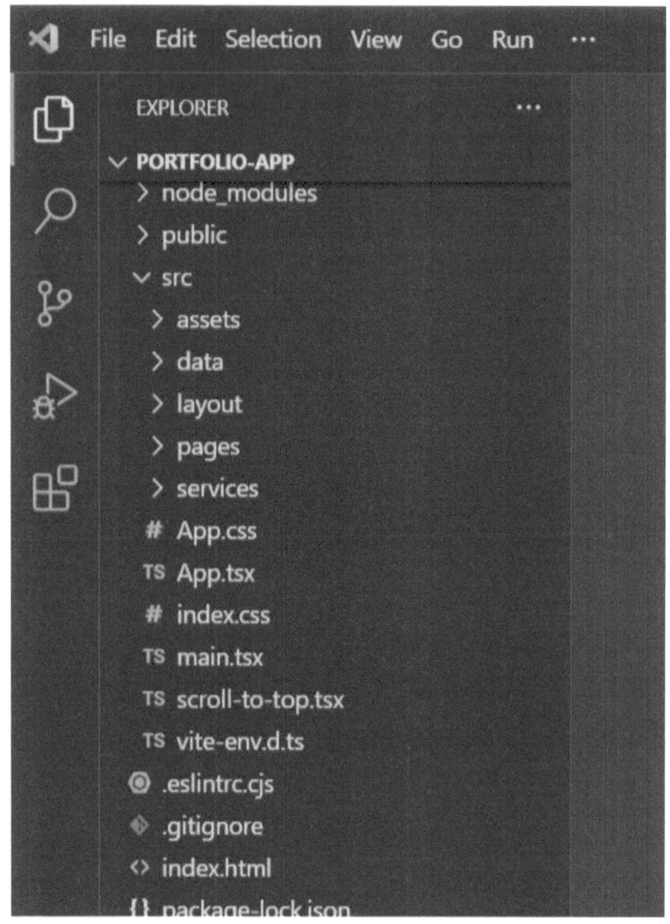

26.2 TSX

```
import { useEffect } from "react";
import { useLocation } from "react-router-dom";

function ScrollToTop() {
```

```
  const { pathname } = useLocation();

  useEffect(() => {
    window.scrollTo(0, 0);
  }, [pathname]);

  return null;
}

export default ScrollToTop;
```

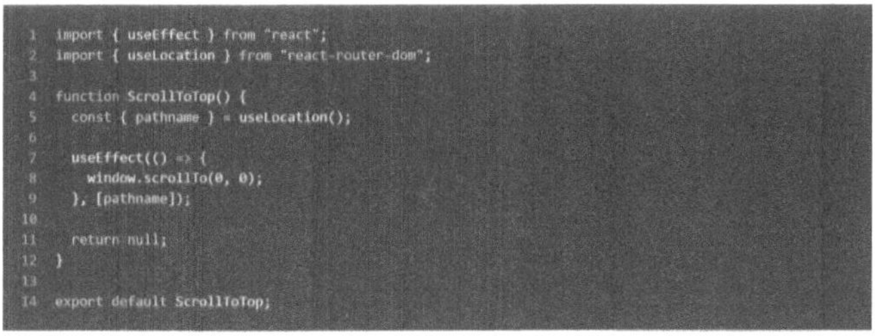

```
1   import { useEffect } from "react";
2   import { useLocation } from "react-router-dom";
3
4   function ScrollToTop() {
5     const { pathname } = useLocation();
6
7     useEffect(() => {
8       window.scrollTo(0, 0);
9     }, [pathname]);
10
11    return null;
12  }
13
14  export default ScrollToTop;
```

26.3 Use It

```
import "./App.css";
import { BrowserRouter, Routes, Route } from
"react-router-dom";
import Footer from "./layout/footer/footer";
import "./layout/top-bar/top-bar";
import TopBar from "./layout/top-bar/top-bar";
import About from "./pages/about/about";
import Contact from "./pages/contact/contact";
import CV from "./pages/cv/cv";
import Home from "./pages/home/home";
import Projects from
"./pages/projects/projects";
import Sidenav from "./layout/sidenav/sidenav";
```

```jsx
import { useState } from "react";
import ScrollToTop from "./scroll-to-top";

function App() {
  const [opened, setOpened] = useState(false);
  return (
    <div>
      <BrowserRouter>
        <ScrollToTop />
        <TopBar opened={opened} setOpened={setOpened} />
        <Sidenav opened={opened} setOpened={setOpened} />
        <main className="main">
          <Routes>
            <Route path="/" element={<Home />} />
            <Route path="/home" element={<Home />} />
            <Route path="/about" element={<About />} />
            <Route path="/cv" element={<CV />} />
            <Route path="/projects" element={<Projects />} />
            <Route path="/contact" element={<Contact />} />
          </Routes>
        </main>
        <Footer />
      </BrowserRouter>
    </div>
  );
}
```

export default App;

```jsx
1   import "./App.css";
2   import { BrowserRouter, Routes, Route } from "react-router-dom";
3
4   import Footer from "./layout/footer/footer";
5   import "./layout/top-bar/top-bar";
6   import TopBar from "./layout/top-bar/top-bar";
7   import About from "./pages/about/about";
8   import Contact from "./pages/contact/contact";
9   import CV from "./pages/cv/cv";
10  import Home from "./pages/home/home";
11  import Projects from "./pages/projects/projects";
12  import Sidenav from "./layout/sidenav/sidenav";
13  import { useState } from "react";
14  import ScrollToTop from "./scroll-to-top";
15
16  function App() {
17    const [opened, setOpened] = useState(false);
18    return (
19      <div>
20        <BrowserRouter>
21          <ScrollToTop />
22          <TopBar opened={opened} setOpened={setOpened} />
23          <Sidenav opened={opened} setOpened={setOpened} />
24          <main className="main">
25            <Routes>
26              <Route path="/" element={<Home />} />
27              <Route path="/home" element={<Home />} />
28              <Route path="/about" element={<About />} />
29              <Route path="/cv" element={<CV />} />
30              <Route path="/projects" element={<Projects />} />
31              <Route path="/contact" element={<Contact />} />
32            </Routes>
33          </main>
34          <Footer />
35        </BrowserRouter>
36      </div>
37    );
38  }
39
40  export default App;
41
```

Conclusion

Congratulations! You have completed the book "React Portfolio App Development". Now you should have created your online portfolio. Remember that learning React is an ongoing process. Practice makes perfect — build your own projects, experiment with the features you learn, and delve into the extensive online resources. Thank you for joining me in my exploration of React. I wish you the best of luck on your programming journey. Good luck with your career and your personal brand and see you in other topics.

— Abdelfattah Ragab

Media Attribution

Rest during work
Image by pressfoto on Freepik

Free vector modern hotel landing page template with photo
Image by Freepik

Free PSD landing page for online fashion sale
Image by Freepik

Travel booking app
Image by pikisuperstar on Freepik

Don't miss out!

Receive an email when Abdelfattah Ragab publishes a new book. It's free and without obligation.

Also by Abdelfattah Ragab

- Responsive Layouts: Flex, Grid and Multi-Column
- Angular Portfolio App Development
- Stripe Integration in Angular
- Angular for Kids
- Angular for Beginners

About the Author

Abdelfattah Ragab is a professional software developer with more than 20 years of experience.
https://abdelfattah-ragab.com

About the Publisher

Abdelfattah Ragab is a highly qualified and experienced software developer with over 20 years of experience in the industry. Specializing in front-end development, Abdelfattah Ragab has a deep understanding of Angular, JavaScript, TypeScript, HTML and CSS. Read more at https://abdelfattah-ragab.com

www.ingramcontent.com/pod-product-compliance
Lightning Source LLC
LaVergne TN
LVHW040015200726
843493LV00005B/1274